Mediterranean Diet Cookbook with Pictures:

Easy Recipes for Beginners with Tips & Tricks to Change your Weight and Lifestyle with an Easy 30-day Meal Plan! Full Color Edition.

Jessica Rossi

Table of Contents

MEDITERRANEAN DIET SHOPPING LIST

STAPLES

Oils
- [ ] Olive Oil
- [ ] Extra-virgin olive oil

Vinegar
- [ ] Balsamic
- [ ] Red wine
- [ ] White wine

A variety of dried herbs & spices
- [ ] Basil
- [ ] Parsley
- [ ] Oregano
- [ ] Cayenne pepper
- [ ] Cinnamon
- [ ] Cloves
- [ ] Cumin
- [ ] Coriander
- [ ] Dill
- [ ] Fennel seed
- [ ] Ginger
- [ ] Rosemary
- [ ] Red and white wine
- [ ] Garlic

MEAT & SEAFOOD

- [ ] Clams
- [ ] Cod
- [ ] Crab meat
- [ ] Halibut
- [ ] Mussels
- [ ] Salmon
- [ ] Scallops
- [ ] Shrimp
- [ ] Tilapia
- [ ] Tuna
- [ ] Chicken breast*
- [ ] Chicken thighs*
- [ ] Lean red meat**

CANNED & PACKAGED

- [ ] Olives
- [ ] Canned Tomatoes

Dried & canned beans
- [ ] Cannellini beans
- [ ] Navy beans
- [ ] Chickpeas
- [ ] Black beans
- [ ] Kidney beans
- [ ] Lentils
- [ ] Canned tuna

Whole Grains
- [ ] Whole grain pasta
- [ ] Bulgur
- [ ] Whole wheat couscous
- [ ] Quinoa
- [ ] Brown rice
- [ ] Barley
- [ ] Faro
- [ ] Polenta
- [ ] Oats
- [ ] Whole wheat bread or pita
- [ ] Whole grain crackers

Nuts & seeds
- [ ] Almonds
- [ ] Hazelnuts
- [ ] Pine nuts
- [ ] Walnuts
- [ ] Cashews
- [ ] Sunflower seeds
- [ ] Sesame seeds

REFRIGERATED

Cheese
- [ ] Cream cheese
- [ ] Feta
- [ ] Goat cheese
- [ ] Mozzarella
- [ ] Parmesan
- [ ] Ricotta
- [ ] Low-fat milk
- [ ] Plain or Greek yogurt
- [ ] Eggs

PRODUCE

- [ ] Apples
- [ ] Artichokes
- [ ] Asparagus
- [ ] Avocado
- [ ] Bananas
- [ ] Beets
- [ ] Bell peppers
- [ ] Berries (all types)
- [ ] Broccoli
- [ ] Brussels sprouts
- [ ] Cabbage
- [ ] Carrots
- [ ] Celery
- [ ] Cherries
- [ ] Cucumbers
- [ ] Dates
- [ ] Eggplant
- [ ] Fennel
- [ ] Figs
- [ ] Grapes
- [ ] Green beans
- [ ] Kiwi
- [ ] Leafy greens
- [ ] Lemons
- [ ] Lettuce
- [ ] Limes
- [ ] Melons
- [ ] Mushrooms
- [ ] Nectarines
- [ ] Onions
- [ ] Oranges
- [ ] Peas
- [ ] Peaches
- [ ] Pears
- [ ] Plums
- [ ] Pomegranate
- [ ] Potatoes
- [ ] Shallots
- [ ] Spinach
- [ ] Squash
- [ ] Tomatoes
- [ ] Zucchini

* In moderation, once to twice per week
** On rare occasions, once to twice monthly

emeals

The 30-Day Meal Plan

	Breakfast	Lunch	Dinner	Total Calories
DAY 1	Spinach and Egg Breakfast Wraps Calories:434	Cherry, Plum, Artichoke, and Cheese Board- Calories: 417	Cioppino (Seafood Tomato Stew) Calories: 221	**1072**
DAY 2	Pumpkin Pie Parfait Calories: 263	Vegetable and Cheese Lavash Pizza Calories: 431	Lemon Grilled Shrimp Calories: 401	**1095**
DAY 3	Mediterranean Eggs (Shakshuka) Calories: 223	Dulse, Avocado, and Tomato Pitas Calories: 412	Avocado Shrimp Ceviche Calories: 496	**1131**
DAY 4	Ricotta Toast with Strawberries Calories: 264	Slow Cooked Turkey and Brown Rice Calories: 499	Lemony Shrimp with Orzo Salad Calories: 565	**1328**
DAY 5	Egg Bake Calories: 240	Cherry, Apricot, and Pecan Brown Rice Bowl-Calories: 451	Garlic Shrimp with Mushrooms Calories: 619	**1310**
DAY 6	Creamy Peach Smoothie Calories: 212	Baked Rolled Oat with Pears and Pecans Calories: 479	Fried Cod Fillets Calories: 333	**1024**
DAY 7	Cauliflower Breakfast Porridge Calories: 381	Mushroom-Pesto Baked Pizza Calories: 348	Cod with Parsley Pistou Calories: 580	**1309**
DAY 8	Apple Compote Calories: 246	Green Veggie Sandwiches Calories: 617	Spicy Grilled Shrimp with Lemon Wedges Calories: 163	**1026**
DAY 9	Tomato and Egg Scramble Calories: 260	Papaya, Jicama, and Peas Rice Bowl Calories: 446	Mediterranean Braised Cod with Vegetables Calories: 332	**1038**
DAY 10	Blueberry Smoothie Calories: 459	Potato Curry Calories: 398	Lemon-Parsley Swordfish Calories: 396	**1253**
DAY 11	Egg Bake Calories: 240	Macadamia Pork Calories: 436	Watermelon and Blueberry Salad Calories: 238	**914**
DAY 12	Creamy Peach Smoothie Calories: 212	Beef Kebabs with Onion and Pepper Calories: 485	Vegetable and Cheese Lavash Pizza Calories: 431	**1128**
DAY 13	Cauliflower Breakfast Porridge Calories: 381	Greek-Style Lamb Burgers Calories: 345	Pizza Pockets Calories: 375	**1101**
DAY 14	Pumpkin Pie Parfait Calories: 263	Chicken Cacciatore Calories: 520	Pecan and Carrot Cake Calories: 255	**1038**

DAY 15	Spinach and Egg Breakfast Wraps Calories:434	Cherry, Plum, Artichoke, and Cheese Board- Calories: 417	Lemony Shrimp with Orzo Salad Calories: 565	**1416**
DAY 16	Pumpkin Pie Parfait Calories: 263	Vegetable and Cheese Lavash Pizza Calories: 431	Garlic Shrimp with Mushrooms Calories: 619	**1313**
DAY 17	Mediterranean Eggs (Shakshuka) Calories: 223	Dulse, Avocado, and Tomato Pitas Calories: 412	Fried Cod Fillets Calories: 333	**968**
DAY 18	Ricotta Toast with Strawberries Calories: 264	Slow Cooked Turkey and Brown Rice Calories: 499	Lemon-Parsley Swordfish Calories: 396	**1159**
DAY 19	Egg Bake Calories: 240	Cherry, Apricot, and Pecan Brown Rice Bowl-Calories: 451	Watermelon and Blueberry Salad Calories: 238	**929**
DAY 20	Creamy Peach Smoothie Calories: 212	Baked Rolled Oat with Pears and Pecans Calories: 479	Vegetable and Cheese Lavash Pizza Calories: 431	**1122**
DAY 21	Cauliflower Breakfast Porridge Calories: 381	Mushroom-Pesto Baked Pizza Calories: 348	Fried Cod Fillets Calories: 333	**1062**
DAY 22	Peanut Butter and Chocolate Balls Calories: 146	Green Veggie Sandwiches Calories: 617	Rice and Blueberry Stuffed Sweet Potatoes Calories: 393	**1156**
DAY 23	Tomato and Egg Scramble Calories: 260	Papaya, Jicama, and Peas Rice Bowl Calories: 446	Pizza Pockets Calories: 375	**1081**
DAY 24	Blueberry Smoothie Calories: 459	Brown Rice Pilaf with Pistachios and Raisins Calories: 264	Pecan and Carrot Cake Calories: 255	**978**
DAY 25	Egg Bake Calories: 240	Black Bean Chili with Mangoes Calories: 430	Cod with Parsley Pistou Calories: 580	**1250**
DAY 26	Creamy Peach Smoothie Calories: 212	Beef Kebabs with Onion and Pepper Calories: 485	Spicy Grilled Shrimp with Lemon Wedges Calories: 163	**860**
DAY 27	Cauliflower Breakfast Porridge Calories: 381	Rice and Blueberry Stuffed Sweet Potatoes Calories: 393	Mediterranean Braised Cod with Vegetables Calories: 332	**1106**
DAY 28	Pumpkin Pie Parfait Calories: 263	Chicken Cacciatore Calories: 520	Cioppino (Seafood Tomato Stew) Calories: 221	**1004**
DAY 29	Tomato and Egg Scramble Calories: 260	Cherry, Plum, Artichoke, and Cheese Board- Calories: 417	Lemon Grilled Shrimp Calories: 401	**1078**
DAY 30	Pecan and Carrot Cake Calories: 255	Vegetable and Cheese Lavash Pizza Calories: 431	Avocado Shrimp Ceviche Calories: 496	**1182**

Breakfasts

Spinach and Egg Breakfast Wraps

Prep time: 10 minutes | Cook time: 7 minutes | Serves 2

1 tablespoon olive oil
¼ cup minced onion
3 to 4 tablespoons minced sun-dried tomatoes in olive oil and herbs
3 large eggs, whisked
1½ cups packed baby spinach
1 ounce (28 g) crumbled feta cheese
Salt, to taste
2 (8-inch) whole-wheat tortillas

1. Heat the olive oil in a large skillet over medium-high heat.
2. Sauté the onion and tomatoes for about 3 minutes, stirring occasionally, until softened.
3. Reduce the heat to medium. Add the whisked eggs and stir-fry for 1 to 2 minutes.
4. Stir in the baby spinach and scatter with the crumbled feta cheese. Season as needed with salt.
5. Remove the egg mixture from the heat to a plate. Set aside.
6. Working in batches, place 2 tortillas on a microwave-safe dish and microwave for about 20 seconds to make them warm.
7. Spoon half of the egg mixture into each tortilla. Fold them in half and roll up, then serve.

Per Serving

calories: 434 | fat: 28.1g | protein: 17.2g | carbs: 30.8g | fiber: 6.0g | sodium: 551mg

Pumpkin Pie Parfait

Prep time: 5 minutes | Cook time: 0 minutes | Serves 4

1 (15-ounce / 425-g) can pure pumpkin purée
4 teaspoons honey
1 teaspoon pumpkin pie spice
¼ teaspoon ground cinnamon
2 cups plain Greek yogurt
1 cup honey granola

1. Combine the pumpkin purée, honey, pumpkin pie spice, and cinnamon in a large bowl and stir to mix well.
2. Cover the bowl with plastic wrap and chill in the refrigerator for at least 2 hours.
3. Make the parfaits: Layer each parfait glass with ¼ cup pumpkin mixture in the bottom. Top with ¼ cup of yogurt and scatter each top with ¼ cup of honey granola. Repeat the layers until the glasses are full.
4. Serve immediately.

Per Serving

calories: 263 | fat: 8.9g | protein: 15.3g | carbs: 34.6g | fiber: 6.0g | sodium: 91mg

Mediterranean Eggs (Shakshuka)

Prep time: 5 minutes | Cook time: 20 minutes | Serves 4

2 tablespoons extra-virgin olive oil
1 cup chopped shallots
1 teaspoon garlic powder
1 cup finely diced potato
1 cup chopped red bell peppers
1 (14.5-ounce/ 411-g) can diced tomatoes, drained
¼ teaspoon ground cardamom
¼ teaspoon paprika
¼ teaspoon turmeric
4 large eggs
¼ cup chopped fresh cilantro

1. Preheat the oven to 350ºF (180ºC).
2. Heat the olive oil in an ovenproof skillet over medium-high heat until it shimmers.
3. Add the shallots and sauté for about 3 minutes, stirring occasionally, until fragrant.
4. Fold in the garlic powder, potato, and bell peppers and stir to combine.
5. Cover and cook for 10 minutes, stirring frequently.
6. Add the tomatoes, cardamon, paprika, and turmeric and mix well.
7. When the mixture begins to bubble, remove from the heat and crack the eggs into the skillet.
8. Transfer the skillet to the preheated oven and bake for 5 to 10 minutes, or until the egg whites are set and the yolks are cooked to your liking.
9. Remove from the oven and garnish with the cilantro before serving.

Per Serving

calories: 223 | fat: 11.8g | protein: 9.1g | carbs: 19.5g | fiber: 3.0g | sodium: 277mg

Ricotta Toast with Strawberries

Prep time: 10 minutes | Cook time: 0 minutes | Serves 2

½ cup crumbled ricotta cheese
1 tablespoon honey, plus additional as needed
Pinch of sea salt, plus additional as needed
4 slices of whole-grain bread, toasted
1 cup sliced fresh strawberries
4 large fresh basil leaves, sliced into thin shreds

1. Mix together the cheese, honey, and salt in a small bowl until well incorporated.
2. Taste and add additional salt and honey as needed.
3. Spoon 2 tablespoons of the cheese mixture onto each slice of bread and spread it all over.
4. Sprinkle the sliced strawberry and basil leaves on top before serving.

Per Serving

calories: 274 | fat: 7.9g | protein: 15.1g | carbs: 39.8g | fiber: 5.0g | sodium: 322mg

6

Egg Bake

Prep time: 10 minutes | Cook time: 30 minutes | Serves 2

1 tablespoon olive oil
1 slice whole-grain bread
4 large eggs
3 tablespoons unsweetened almond milk
½ teaspoon onion powder
¼ teaspoon garlic powder
¾ cup chopped cherry tomatoes
¼ teaspoon salt
Pinch freshly ground black pepper

1. Preheat the oven to 375ºF (190ºC).
2. Coat two ramekins with the olive oil and transfer to a baking sheet. Line the bottom of each ramekin with ½ of bread slice.
3. In a medium bowl, whisk together the eggs, almond milk, onion powder, garlic powder, tomatoes, salt, and pepper until well combined.
4. Pour the mixture evenly into two ramekins. Bake in the preheated oven for 30 minutes, or until the eggs are completely set.
5. Cool for 5 minutes before serving.

Per Serving

calories: 240 | fat: 17.4g | protein: 9.0g | carbs: 12.2g | fiber: 2.8g | sodium: 396mg

Creamy Peach Smoothie

Prep time: 15 minutes | Cook time: 0 minutes | Serves 2

2 cups packed frozen peaches, partially thawed
½ ripe avocado
½ cup plain or vanilla Greek yogurt
2 tablespoons flax meal
1 tablespoon honey
1 teaspoon orange extract
1 teaspoon vanilla extract

1. Place all the ingredients in a blender and blend until completely mixed and smooth.
2. Divide the mixture into two bowls and serve immediately.

Per Serving

calories: 212 | fat: 13.1g | protein: 6.0g | carbs: 22.5g | fiber: 7.2g | sodium: 40mg

Blueberry Smoothie

Prep time: 5 minutes | Cook time: 0 minutes | Serves 1

1 cup unsweetened almond milk, plus additional as needed
¼ cup frozen blueberries
2 tablespoons unsweetened almond butter
1 tablespoon extra-virgin olive oil
1 tablespoon ground flaxseed or chia seeds
1 to 2 teaspoons maple syrup
½ teaspoon vanilla extract
¼ teaspoon ground cinnamon

1. Blend all the ingredients in a blender until smooth and creamy.
2. You can add additional almond milk to reach your preferred consistency as needed. Serve immediately.

Per Serving

calories: 459 | fat: 40.1g | protein: 8.9g | carbs: 20.0g | fiber: 10.1g | sodium: 147mg

Cauliflower Breakfast Porridge

Prep time: 5 minutes | Cook time: 5 minutes | Serves 2

2 cups riced cauliflower
¾ cup unsweetened almond milk
4 tablespoons extra-virgin olive oil, divided
2 teaspoons grated fresh orange peel (from ½ orange)
½ teaspoon almond extract or vanilla extract
½ teaspoon ground cinnamon
⅛ teaspoon salt
4 tablespoons chopped walnuts, divided
1 to 2 teaspoons maple syrup (optional)

1. Place the riced cauliflower, almond milk, 2 tablespoons of olive oil, orange peel, almond extract, cinnamon, and salt in a medium saucepan. Stir to incorporate and bring the mixture to a boil over medium-high heat, stirring.
2. Remove from the heat and add 2 tablespoons of chopped walnuts and maple syrup (if desired).Stir again and divide the porridge into bowls. Sprinkle each bowl evenly with remaining 2 tablespoons of walnuts and olive oil.

Per Serving

calories: 381 | fat: 37.8g | protein: 5.2g | carbs: 10.9g | fiber: 4.0g | sodium: 228mg

Morning Overnight Oats with Raspberries

Prep time: 5 minutes | Cook time: 0 minutes | Serves 2

⅔ cup unsweetened almond milk
¼ cup raspberries
⅓ cup rolled oats
1 teaspoon honey
¼ teaspoon turmeric
⅛ teaspoon ground cinnamon
Pinch ground cloves

1. Place the almond milk, raspberries, rolled oats, honey, turmeric, cinnamon, and cloves in a mason jar. Cover and shake to combine. Transfer to the refrigerator for at least 8 hours, preferably 24 hours. Serve chilled.

Per Serving

calories: 81 | fat: 1.9g | protein: 2.1g | carbs: 13.8g | fiber: 3.0g | sodium: 97mg

Tomato and Egg Scramble

Prep time: 10 minutes | Cook time: 20 minutes | Serves 4

2 tablespoons extra-virgin olive oil
¼ cup finely minced red onion
1½ cups chopped fresh tomatoes
2 garlic cloves, minced
½ teaspoon dried thyme
½ teaspoon dried oregano
8 large eggs
½ teaspoon salt
¼ teaspoon freshly ground black pepper
¾ cup crumbled feta cheese
¼ cup chopped fresh mint leaves

1. Heat the olive oil in a large skillet over medium heat.
2. Sauté the red onion and tomatoes in the hot skillet for 10 to 12 minutes, or until the tomatoes are softened. Stir in the garlic, thyme, and oregano and sauté for 2 to 4 minutes, or until the garlic is fragrant. Meanwhile, beat the eggs with the salt and pepper in a medium bowl until frothy. Pour the beaten eggs into the skillet and reduce the heat to low. Scramble for 3 to 4 minutes, stirring constantly, or until the eggs are set. Remove from the heat and scatter with the feta cheese and mint. Serve warm.

Per Serving

calories: 260 | fat: 21.9g | protein: 10.2g | carbs: 5.8g | fiber: 1.0g | sodium: 571mg

Sides, Salads, and Soups

Sumptuous Greek Vegetable Salad

Prep time: 20 minutes | Cook time: 0 minutes | Serves 6

Salad:
1 (15-ounce / 425-g) can chickpeas, drained and rinsed
1 (14-ounce / 397-g) can artichoke hearts, drained and halved
1 head Bibb lettuce, chopped (about 2½ cups)
1 cucumber, peeled deseeded, and chopped (about 1½ cups)
1½ cups grape tomatoes, halved
¼ cup chopped basil leaves
½ cup sliced black olives
½ cup cubed feta cheese

Dressing:
1 tablespoon freshly squeezed lemon juice (from about ½ small lemon)
¼ teaspoon freshly ground black pepper
1 tablespoon chopped fresh oregano
2 tablespoons extra-virgin olive oil
1 tablespoon red wine vinegar
1 teaspoon honey

1. Combine the ingredients for the salad in a large salad bowl, then toss to combine well.
2. Combine the ingredients for the dressing in a small bowl, then stir to mix well.
3. Dress the salad and serve immediately.

Per Serving

calories: 165 | fat: 8.1g | protein: 7.2g | carbs: 17.9g | fiber: 7.0g | sodium: 337mg

Brussels Sprout and Apple Slaw

Prep time: 15 minutes | Cook time: 0 minutes | Serves 4

Salad:
1 pound (454 g) Brussels sprouts, stem ends removed and sliced thinly
1 apple, cored and sliced thinly
½ red onion, sliced thinly
Dressing:
1 teaspoon Dijon mustard
2 teaspoons apple cider vinegar
1 tablespoon raw honey
1 cup plain coconut yogurt
1 teaspoon sea salt
For Garnish:
½ cup pomegranate seeds
½ cup chopped toasted hazelnuts

1. Combine the ingredients for the salad in a large salad bowl, then toss to combine well.
2. Combine the ingredients for the dressing in a small bowl, then stir to mix well.
3. Dress the salad let sit for 10 minutes. Serve with pomegranate seeds and toasted hazelnuts on top.

Per Serving

calories: 248 | fat: 11.2g | protein: 12.7g | carbs: 29.9g | fiber: 8.0g | sodium: 645mg

Butternut Squash and Cauliflower Soup

Prep time: 15 minutes | Cook time: 4 hours | Serves 4 to 6

1 pound (454 g) butternut squash, peeled and cut into 1-inch cubes
1 small head cauliflower, cut into 1-inch pieces
1 onion, sliced
2 cups unsweetened coconut milk
1 tablespoon curry powder
½ cup no-added-sugar apple juice
4 cups low-sodium vegetable soup
2 tablespoons coconut oil
1 teaspoon sea salt
¼ teaspoon freshly ground white pepper
¼ cup chopped fresh cilantro, divided

1. Combine all the ingredients, except for the cilantro, in the slow cooker. Stir to mix well.
2. Cook on high heat for 4 hours or until the vegetables are tender.
3. Pour the soup in a food processor, then pulse until creamy and smooth.
4. Pour the puréed soup in a large serving bowl and garnish with cilantro before serving.

Per Serving

calories: 415 | fat: 30.8g | protein: 10.1g | carbs: 29.9g | fiber: 7.0g | sodium: 1386mg

Cherry, Plum, Artichoke, and Cheese Board

Prep time: 15 minutes | Cook time: 0 minutes | Serves 4

2 cups rinsed cherries
2 cups rinsed and sliced plums
2 cups rinsed carrots, cut into sticks
1 cup canned low-sodium artichoke hearts, rinsed and drained
1 cup cubed feta cheese

1. Arrange all the ingredients in separated portions on a clean board or a large tray, then serve with spoons, knife, and forks.

Per Serving

calories: 417 | fat: 13.8g | protein: 20.1g | carbs: 56.2g | fiber: 3.0g | sodium: 715mg

Artichoke and Arugula Salad

Prep time: 10 minutes | Cook time: 0 minutes | Serves 6

Salad:
6 canned oil-packed artichoke hearts, sliced
6 cups baby arugula leaves
6 fresh olives, pitted and chopped
1 cup cherry tomatoes, sliced in half

Dressing:
1 teaspoon Dijon mustard
2 tablespoons balsamic vinegar
1 clove garlic, minced
2 tablespoons extra-virgin olive oil

For Garnish:
4 fresh basil leaves, thinly sliced

1. Combine the ingredients for the salad in a large salad bowl, then toss to combine well. Combine the ingredients for the dressing in a small bowl, then stir to mix well.
2. Dress the salad, then serve with basil leaves on top.

Per Serving

calories: 134 | fat: 12.1g | protein: 1.6g | carbs: 6.2g | fiber: 3.0g| sodium: 65mg

Baby Potato and Olive Salad

Prep time: 10 minutes | Cook time: 20 minutes | Serves 6

2 pounds (907 g) baby potatoes, cut into 1-inch cubes
1 tablespoon low-sodium olive brine
3 tablespoons freshly squeezed lemon juice (from about 1 medium lemon)
¼ teaspoon kosher salt
3 tablespoons extra-virgin olive oil
½ cup sliced olives
2 tablespoons torn fresh mint
1 cup sliced celery (about 2 stalks)
2 tablespoons chopped fresh oregano

1. Put the tomatoes in a saucepan, then pour in enough water to submerge the tomatoes about 1 inch. Bring to a boil over high heat, then reduce the heat to medium-low. Simmer for 14 minutes or until the potatoes are soft. Meanwhile, combine the olive brine, lemon juice, salt, and olive oil in a small bow. Stir to mix well.
2. Transfer the cooked tomatoes in a colander, then rinse with running cold water. Pat dry with paper towels. Transfer the tomatoes in a large salad bowl, then drizzle with olive brine mixture. Spread with remaining ingredients and toss to combine well. Serve immediately.

Per Serving

calories: 220 | fat: 6.1g | protein: 4.3g | carbs: 39.2g | fiber: 5.0g | sodium: 231mg

Barley, Parsley, and Pea Salad

Prep time: 10 minutes | Cook time: 10 minutes | Serves 4

2 cups water
1 cup quick-cooking barley
1 small bunch flat-leaf parsley, chopped (about 1 to 1½ cups)
2 cups sugar snap pea pods
Juice of 1 lemon
½ small red onion, diced
2 tablespoons extra-virgin olive oil
Sea salt and freshly ground pepper, to taste

1. Pour the water in a saucepan. Bring to a boil. Add the barley to the saucepan, then put the lid on.
2. Reduce the heat to low. Simmer the barley for 10 minutes or until the liquid is absorbed, then let sit for 5 minutes.
3. Open the lid, then transfer the barley in a colander and rinse under cold running water.
4. Pour the barley in a large salad bowl and add the remaining ingredients. Toss to combine well.
5. Serve immediately.

Per Serving

calories: 152 | fat: 7.4g | protein: 3.7g | carbs: 19.3g | fiber: 4.7g| sodium: 20mg

Cheesy Peach and Walnut Salad

Prep time: 10 minutes | Cook time: 0 minutes | Serves 1

1 ripe peach, pitted and sliced
¼ cup chopped walnuts, toasted
¼ cup shredded Parmesan cheese
1 teaspoon raw honey
Zest of 1 lemon
1 tablespoon chopped fresh mint

1. Combine the peach, walnut, and cheese in a medium bowl, then drizzle with honey. Spread the lemon zest and mint on top. Toss to combine everything well. Serve immediately.

Per Serving

calories: 373 | fat: 26.4g | protein: 12.9g | carbs: 27.0g | fiber: 4.7g | sodium: 453mg

Greek Chicken, Tomato, and Olive Salad

Prep time: 10 minutes | Cook time: 0 minutes | Serves 2

Salad:
2 grilled boneless, skinless chicken breasts, sliced (about 1 cup)
10 cherry tomatoes, halved
8 pitted Kalamata olives, halved
½ cup thinly sliced red onion
Dressing:
¼ cup balsamic vinegar
1 teaspoon freshly squeezed lemon juice
¼ teaspoon sea salt
¼ teaspoon freshly ground black pepper
2 teaspoons extra-virgin olive oil
For Serving:
2 cups roughly chopped romaine lettuce
½ cup crumbled feta cheese

1. Combine the ingredients for the salad in a large bowl. Toss to combine well. Combine the ingredients for the dressing in a small bowl. Stir to mix well. Pour the dressing the bowl of salad, then toss to coat well. Wrap the bowl in plastic and refrigerate for at least 2 hours.
2. Remove the bowl from the refrigerator. Spread the lettuce on a large plate, then top with marinated salad. Scatter the salad with feta cheese and serve immediately.

Per Serving

calories: 328 | fat: 16.9g | protein: 27.6g | carbs: 15.9g | fiber: 3.1g| sodium: 1102mg

Ritzy Summer Fruit Salad

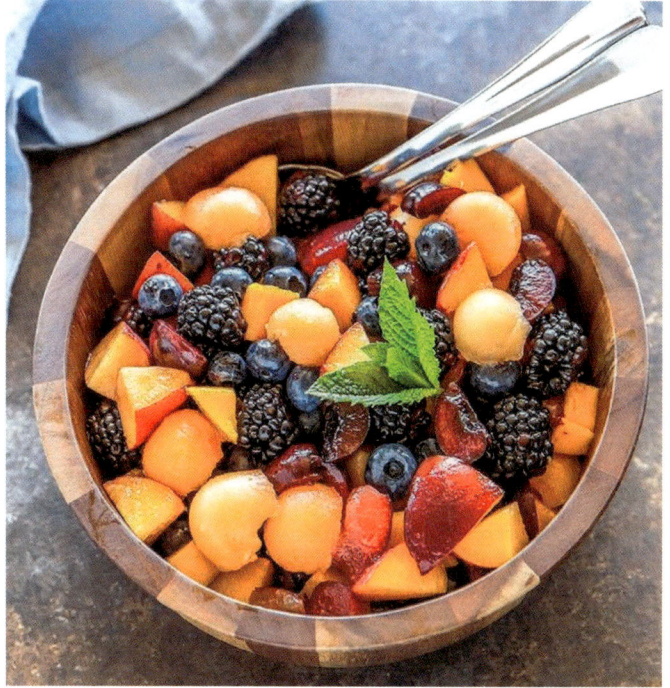

Prep time: 10 minutes | Cook time: 0 minutes | Serves 8

Salad:
1 cup fresh blueberries
2 cups cubed cantaloupe
2 cups red seedless grapes
1 cup sliced fresh strawberries
2 cups cubed honeydew melon
Zest of 1 large lime
½ cup unsweetened toasted coconut flakes
Dressing:
¼ cup raw honey
Juice of 1 large lime
¼ teaspoon sea salt
½ cup extra-virgin olive oil

1. Combine the ingredients for the salad in a large salad bowl, then toss to combine well. Combine the ingredients for the dressing in a small bowl, then stir to mix well.
2. Dress the salad and serve immediately.

Per Serving

calories: 242 | fat: 15.5g | protein: 1.3g | carbs: 28.0g | fiber: 2.4g | sodium: 90mg

Sandwiches, Pizzas, and Wraps

Mashed Grape Tomato Pizzas

Prep time: 10 minutes | Cook time: 20 minutes | Serves 6

3 cups grape tomatoes, halved
1 teaspoon chopped fresh thyme leaves
2 garlic cloves, minced
¼ teaspoon kosher salt
¼ teaspoon freshly ground black pepper
1 tablespoon extra-virgin olive oil
¾ cup shredded Parmesan cheese
6 whole-wheat pita breads

1. Preheat the oven to 425ºF (220ºC).
2. Combine the tomatoes, thyme, garlic, salt, ground black pepper, and olive oil in a baking pan.
3. Roast in the preheated oven for 20 minutes. Remove the pan from the oven, mash the tomatoes with a spatula and stir to mix well halfway through the cooking time.
4. Meanwhile, divide and spread the cheese over each pita bread, then place the bread in a separate baking pan and roast in the oven for 5 minutes or until golden brown and the cheese melts.
5. Transfer the pita bread onto a large plate, then top with the roasted mashed tomatoes. Serve immediately.

Per Serving

calories: 140 | fat: 5.1g | protein: 6.2g | carbs: 16.9g | fiber: 2.0g | sodium: 466mg

Vegetable and Cheese Lavash Pizza

Prep time: 15 minutes | Cook time: 11 minutes | Serves 4

2 (12 by 9-inch) lavash breads
2 tablespoons extra-virgin olive oil
10 ounces (284 g) frozen spinach, thawed and squeezed dry
1 cup shredded fontina cheese
1 tomato, cored and cut into ½-inch pieces
½ cup pitted large green olives, chopped
¼ teaspoon red pepper flakes
3 garlic cloves, minced
¼ teaspoon sea salt
¼ teaspoon ground black pepper
½ cup grated Parmesan cheese

1. Preheat oven to 475ºF (246ºC).
2. Brush the lavash breads with olive oil, then place them on two baking sheet. Heat in the preheated oven for 4 minutes or until lightly browned. Flip the breads halfway through the cooking time.
3. Meanwhile, combine the spinach, fontina cheese, tomato pieces, olives, red pepper flakes, garlic, salt, and black pepper in a large bowl. Stir to mix well.
4. Remove the lavash bread from the oven and sit them on two large plates, spread them with the spinach mixture, then scatter with the Parmesan cheese on top.
5. Bake in the oven for 7 minutes or until the cheese melts and well browned. Slice and serve warm.

Per Serving

calories: 431 | fat: 21.5g | protein: 20.0g | carbs: 38.4g | fiber: 2.5g | sodium: 854mg

Dulse, Avocado, and Tomato Pitas

Prep time: 10 minutes | Cook time: 30 minutes | Makes 4 pitas

2 teaspoons coconut oil
½ cup dulse, picked through and separated
Ground black pepper, to taste
2 avocados, sliced
2 tablespoons lime juice
¼ cup chopped cilantro
2 scallions, white and light green parts, sliced
Sea salt, to taste
4 (8-inch) whole wheat pitas, sliced in half
4 cups chopped romaine
4 plum tomatoes, sliced

1. Heat the coconut oil in a nonstick skillet over medium heat until melted. Add the dulse and sauté for 5 minutes or until crispy. Sprinkle with ground black pepper and turn off the heat. Set aside. Put the avocado, lime juice, cilantro, and scallions in a food processor and sprinkle with salt and ground black pepper. Pulse to combine well until smooth.
2. Toast the pitas in a baking pan in the oven for 1 minute until soft.
3. Transfer the pitas to a clean work surface and open. Spread the avocado mixture over the pitas, then top with dulse, romaine, and tomato slices. Serve immediately.

Per Serving (1 pita)

calories: 412 | fat: 18.7g | protein: 9.1g | carbs: 56.1g | fiber: 12.5g | sodium: 695mg

Greek Vegetable Salad Pita

Prep time: 10 minutes | Cook time: 0 minutes | Serves 4

½ cup baby spinach leaves
½ small red onion, thinly sliced
½ small cucumber, deseeded and chopped
1 tomato, chopped
1 cup chopped romaine lettuce
1 tablespoon extra-virgin olive oil
½ tablespoon red wine vinegar
1 teaspoon Dijon mustard
1 tablespoon crumbled feta cheese
Sea salt and freshly ground pepper, to taste
1 whole-wheat pita

1. Combine all the ingredients, except for the pita, in a large bowl. Toss to mix well. Stuff the pita with the salad, then serve immediately.

Per Serving

calories: 137 | fat: 8.1g | protein: 3.1g | carbs: 14.3g | fiber: 2.4g | sodium: 166mg

Artichoke and Cucumber Hoagies

Prep time: 10 minutes | Cook time: 15 minutes | Makes 1

1 (12-ounce / 340-g) whole grain baguette, sliced in half horizontally
1 cup frozen and thawed artichoke hearts, roughly chopped
1 cucumber, sliced
2 tomatoes, sliced
1 red bell pepper, sliced
⅓ cup Kalamata olives, pitted and chopped
¼ small red onion, thinly sliced
Sea salt and ground black pepper, to taste
2 tablespoons pesto
Balsamic vinegar, to taste

1. rrange the baguette halves on a clean work surface, then cut off the top third from each half. Scoop some insides of the bottom half out and reserve as breadcrumbs.
2. Toast the baguette in a baking pan in the oven for 1 minute to brown lightly. Put the artichokes, cucumber, tomatoes, bell pepper, olives, and onion in a large bowl. Sprinkle with salt and ground black pepper. Toss to combine well.
3. Spread the bottom half of the baguette with the vegetable mixture and drizzle with balsamic vinegar, then smear the cut side of the baguette top with pesto. Assemble the two baguette halves. Wrap the hoagies in parchment paper and let sit for at least an hour before serving.

Per Serving (1 hoagies)

calories: 1263 | fat: 37.7g | protein: 56.3g | carbs: 180.1g | fiber: 37.8g | sodium: 2137mg

Alfalfa Sprout and Nut Rolls

Prep time: 40 minutes | Cook time: 0 minutes | Makes 16 bite-size pieces

1 cup alfalfa sprouts
2 tablespoons Brazil nuts
½ cup chopped fresh cilantro
2 tablespoons flaked coconut
1 garlic clove, minced
2 tablespoons ground flaxseeds
Zest and juice of 1 lemon
Pinch cayenne pepper
Sea salt and freshly ground black pepper, to taste
1 tablespoon melted coconut oil
2 tablespoons water
2 whole-grain wraps

1. Combine all ingredients, except for the wraps, in a food processor, then pulse to combine well until smooth.
2. Unfold the wraps on a clean work surface, then spread the mixture over the wraps.
3. Roll the wraps up and refrigerate for 30 minutes until set.
4. Remove the rolls from the refrigerator and slice into 16 bite-sized pieces, if desired, and serve.

Per Serving (1 piece)

calories: 67 | fat: 7.1g | protein: 2.2g | carbs: 2.9g | fiber: 1.0g | sodium: 61mg

Mini Pork and Cucumber Lettuce Wraps

Prep time: 20 minutes | Cook time: 0 minutes | Makes 12 wraps

8 ounces (227 g) cooked ground pork
1 cucumber, diced
1 tomato, diced
1 red onion, sliced
1 ounce (28 g) low-fat feta cheese, crumbled

Juice of 1 lemon
1 tablespoon extra-virgin olive oil
Sea salt and freshly ground pepper, to taste
12 small, intact iceberg lettuce leaves

1. Combine the ground pork, cucumber, tomato, and onion in a large bowl, then scatter with feta cheese.
2. Drizzle with lemon juice and olive oil, and sprinkle with salt and pepper. Toss to mix well.
3. Unfold the small lettuce leaves on a large plate or several small plates, then divide and top with the pork mixture.
4. Wrap and serve immediately.

Per Serving (1 warp)

calories: 78 | fat: 5.6g | protein: 5.5g | carbs: 1.4g | fiber: 0.3g | sodium: 50mg

Green Veggie Sandwiches

Prep time: 20 minutes | Cook time: 0 minutes | Serves 2

Spread:
1 (15-ounce / 425-g) can cannellini beans, drained and rinsed
⅓ cup packed fresh basil leaves
⅓ cup packed fresh parsley
⅓ cup chopped fresh chives
2 garlic cloves, chopped
Zest and juice of ½ lemon
1 tablespoon apple cider vinegar

Sandwiches:
4 whole-grain bread slices, toasted
8 English cucumber slices
1 large beefsteak tomato, cut into slices
1 large avocado, halved, pitted, and cut into slices
1 small yellow bell pepper, cut into slices
2 handfuls broccoli sprouts
2 handfuls fresh spinach

Make the Spread

1. In a food processor, combine the cannellini beans, basil, parsley, chives, garlic, lemon zest and juice, and vinegar. Pulse a few times, scrape down the sides, and purée until smooth. You may need to scrape down the sides again to incorporate all the basil and parsley. Refrigerate for at least 1 hour to allow the flavors to blend.
1. Assemble the Sandwiches
2. Build your sandwiches by spreading several tablespoons of spread on each slice of bread. Layer two slices of bread with the cucumber, tomato, avocado, bell pepper, broccoli sprouts, and spinach. Top with the remaining bread slices and press down lightly.
3. Serve immediately.

Per Serving

calories: 617 | fat: 21.1g | protein: 28.1g | carbs: 86.1g | fiber: 25.6g | sodium: 593mg

Pizza Pockets

Prep time: 10 minutes | Cook time: 0 minutes | Serves 2

½ cup tomato sauce
½ teaspoon oregano
½ teaspoon garlic powder
½ cup chopped black olives

2 canned artichoke hearts, drained and chopped
2 ounces (57 g) pepperoni, chopped
½ cup shredded Mozzarella cheese
1 whole-wheat pita, halved

1. In a medium bowl, stir together the tomato sauce, oregano, and garlic powder.
2. Add the olives, artichoke hearts, pepperoni, and cheese. Stir to mix.
3. Spoon the mixture into the pita halves and serve.

Per Serving

calories: 375 | fat: 23.5g | protein: 17.1g | carbs: 27.1g | fiber: 6.1g | sodium: 1080mg

Mushroom-Pesto Baked Pizza

Prep time: 5 minutes | Cook time: 15 minutes | Serves 2

1 teaspoon extra-virgin olive oil
½ cup sliced mushrooms
½ red onion, sliced
Salt and freshly ground black pepper

¼ cup store-bought pesto sauce
2 whole-wheat flatbreads
¼ cup shredded Mozzarella cheese

1. Preheat the oven to 350ºF (180ºC). In a small skillet, heat the oil over medium heat. Add the mushrooms and onion, and season with salt and pepper. Sauté for 3 to 5 minutes until the onion and mushrooms begin to soften. Spread 2 tablespoons of pesto on each flatbread. Divide the mushroom-onion mixture between the two flatbreads. Top each with 2 tablespoons of cheese. Place the flatbreads on a baking sheet and bake for 10 to 12 minutes until the cheese is melted and bubbly. Serve warm.

Per Serving

calories: 348 | fat: 23.5g | protein: 14.2g | carbs: 28.1g | fiber: 7.1g | sodium: 792mg

Beans, Grains, and Pastas

Baked Rolled Oat with Pears and Pecans

Prep time: 15 minutes | Cook time: 30 minutes | Serves 6

2 tablespoons coconut oil, melted, plus more for greasing the pan
3 ripe pears, cored and diced
2 cups unsweetened almond milk
1 tablespoon pure vanilla extract
¼ cup pure maple syrup
2 cups gluten-free rolled oats
½ cup raisins
¾ cup chopped pecans
¼ teaspoon ground nutmeg
1 teaspoon ground cinnamon
½ teaspoon ground ginger
¼ teaspoon sea salt

1. Preheat the oven to 350ºF (180ºC). Grease a baking dish with melted coconut oil, then spread the pears in a single layer on the baking dish evenly.
2. Combine the almond milk, vanilla extract, maple syrup, and coconut oil in a bowl. Stir to mix well.
3. Combine the remaining ingredients in a separate large bowl. Stir to mix well. Fold the almond milk mixture in the bowl, then pour the mixture over the pears.
4. Place the baking dish in the preheated oven and bake for 30 minutes or until lightly browned and set.
5. Serve immediately.

Per Serving

calories: 479 | fat: 34.9g | protein: 8.8g | carbs: 50.1g | fiber: 10.8g | sodium: 113mg

Brown Rice Pilaf with Pistachios and Raisins

Prep time: 5 minutes | Cook time: 15 minutes | Serves 6

1 tablespoon extra-virgin olive oil
1 cup chopped onion
½ cup shredded carrot
½ teaspoon ground cinnamon
1 teaspoon ground cumin
2 cups brown rice
1¾ cups pure orange juice
¼ cup water
½ cup shelled pistachios
1 cup golden raisins
½ cup chopped fresh chives

1. Heat the olive oil in a saucepan over medium-high heat until shimmering.
2. Add the onion and sauté for 5 minutes or until translucent.
3. Add the carrots, cinnamon, and cumin, then sauté for 1 minutes or until aromatic.
4. Pour int the brown rice, orange juice, and water. Bring to a boil. Reduce the heat to medium-low and simmer for 7 minutes or until the liquid is almost absorbed.
5. Transfer the rice mixture in a large serving bowl, then spread with pistachios, raisins, and chives. Serve immediately.

Per Serving

calories: 264 | fat: 7.1g | protein: 5.2g | carbs: 48.9g | fiber: 4.0g | sodium: 86mg

Cherry, Apricot, and Pecan Brown Rice Bowl

Prep time: 15 minutes | Cook time: 1 hour 1 minutes | Serves 2

2 tablespoons olive oil
2 green onions, sliced
½ cup brown rice
1 cup low -sodium chicken stock
2 tablespoons dried cherries

4 dried apricots, chopped
2 tablespoons pecans, toasted and chopped
Sea salt and freshly ground pepper, to taste

1. Heat the olive oil in a medium saucepan over medium-high heat until shimmering.
2. Add the green onions and sauté for 1 minutes or until fragrant.
3. Add the rice. Stir to mix well, then pour in the chicken stock.
4. Bring to a boil. Reduce the heat to low. Cover and simmer for 50 minutes or until the brown rice is soft.
5. Add the cherries, apricots, and pecans, and simmer for 10 more minutes or until the fruits are tender.
6. Pour them in a large serving bowl. Fluff with a fork. Sprinkle with sea salt and freshly ground pepper. Serve immediately.

Per Serving

calories: 451 | fat: 25.9g | protein: 8.2g | carbs: 50.4g | fiber: 4.6g | sodium: 122mg

Curry Apple Couscous with Leeks and Pecans

Prep time: 10 minutes | Cook time: 8 minutes | Serves 4

2 teaspoons extra-virgin olive oil
2 leeks, white parts only, sliced
1 apple, diced

2 cups cooked couscous
2 tablespoons curry powder
½ cup chopped pecans

1. Heat the olive oil in a skillet over medium heat until shimmering.
2. Add the leeks and sauté for 5 minutes or until soft.
3. Add the diced apple and cook for 3 more minutes until tender.
4. Add the couscous and curry powder. Stir to combine.
5. Transfer them in a large serving bowl, then mix in the pecans and serve.

Per Serving

calories: 254 | fat: 11.9g | protein: 5.4g | carbs: 34.3g | fiber: 5.9g | sodium: 15mg

Lebanese Flavor Broken Thin Noodles

Prep time: 10 minutes | Cook time: 25 minutes | Serves 6

1 tablespoon extra-virgin olive oil
1 (3-ounce / 85-g) cup vermicelli, broken into 1- to 1½-inch pieces
3 cups shredded cabbage
1 cup brown rice
3 cups low-sodium vegetable soup

½ cup water
2 garlic cloves, mashed
¼ teaspoon sea salt
⅛ teaspoon crushed red pepper flakes
½ cup coarsely chopped cilantro
Fresh lemon slices, for serving

1. Heat the olive oil in a saucepan over medium-high heat until shimmering.
2. Add the vermicelli and sauté for 3 minutes or until toasted.
3. Add the cabbage and sauté for 4 minutes or until tender.
4. Pour in the brown rice, vegetable soup, and water. Add the garlic and sprinkle with salt and red pepper flakes.
5. Bring to a boil over high heat. Reduce the heat to medium low. Put the lid on and simmer for another 10 minutes.
6. Turn off the heat, then let sit for 5 minutes without opening the lid.
7. Pour them on a large serving platter and spread with cilantro. Squeeze the lemon slices over and serve warm.

Per Serving

calories: 127 | fat: 3.1g | protein: 4.2g | carbs: 22.9g | fiber: 3.0g | sodium: 224mg

Lemony Farro and Avocado Bowl

Prep time: 5 minutes | Cook time: 25 minutes | Serves 4

1 tablespoon plus 2 teaspoons extra-virgin olive oil, divided
½ medium onion, chopped
1 carrot, shredded
2 garlic cloves, minced
1 (6-ounce / 170-g) cup pearled farro

2 cups low-sodium vegetable soup
2 avocados, peeled, pitted, and sliced
Zest and juice of 1 small lemon
¼ teaspoon sea salt

1. Heat 1 tablespoon of olive oil in a saucepan over medium-high heat until shimmering.
2. Add the onion and sauté for 5 minutes or until translucent.
3. Add the carrot and garlic and sauté for 1 minute or until fragrant.
4. Add the farro and pour in the vegetable soup. Bring to a boil over high heat. Reduce the heat to low. Put the lid on and simmer for 20 minutes or until the farro is al dente.
5. Transfer the farro in a large serving bowl, then fold in the avocado slices. Sprinkle with lemon zest and salt, then drizzle with lemon juice and 2 teaspoons of olive oil.
6. Stir to mix well and serve immediately.

Per Serving

calories: 210 | fat: 11.1g | protein: 4.2g | carbs: 27.9g | fiber: 7.0g | sodium: 152mg

Rice and Blueberry Stuffed Sweet Potatoes

Prep time: 15 minutes | Cook time: 20 minutes | Serves 4

2 cups cooked wild rice
½ cup dried blueberries
½ cup chopped hazelnuts
½ cup shredded Swiss chard
1 teaspoon chopped fresh thyme
1 scallion, white and green parts, peeled and thinly sliced
Sea salt and freshly ground black pepper, to taste
4 sweet potatoes, baked in the skin until tender

1. Preheat the oven to 400ºF (205ºC).
2. Combine all the ingredients, except for the sweet potatoes, in a large bowl. Stir to mix well.
3. Cut the top third of the sweet potato off length wire, then scoop most of the sweet potato flesh out.
4. Fill the potato with the wild rice mixture, then set the sweet potato on a greased baking sheet.
5. Bake in the preheated oven for 20 minutes or until the sweet potato skin is lightly charred.
6. Serve immediately.

Per Serving

calories: 393 | fat: 7.1g | protein: 10.2g | carbs: 76.9g | fiber: 10.0g | sodium: 93mg

Slow Cooked Turkey and Brown Rice

Prep time: 20 minutes | Cook time: 3 hours 10 minutes | Serves 6

1 tablespoon extra-virgin olive oil
1½ pounds (680 g) ground turkey
2 tablespoons chopped fresh sage, divided
2 tablespoons chopped fresh thyme, divided
1 teaspoon sea salt
½ teaspoon ground black pepper
2 cups brown rice
1 (14-ounce / 397-g) can stewed tomatoes, with the juice
¼ cup pitted and sliced Kalamata olives
3 medium zucchini, sliced thinly
¼ cup chopped fresh flat-leaf parsley
1 medium yellow onion, chopped
1 tablespoon plus 1 teaspoon balsamic vinegar
2 cups low-sodium chicken stock
2 garlic cloves, minced
½ cup grated Parmesan cheese, for serving

1. Heat the olive oil in a nonstick skillet over medium-high heat until shimmering.
2. Add the ground turkey and sprinkle with 1 tablespoon of sage, 1 tablespoon of thyme, salt and ground black pepper.
3. Sauté for 10 minutes or until the ground turkey is lightly browned.
4. Pour them in the slow cooker, then pour in the remaining ingredients, except for the Parmesan. Stir to mix well.
5. Put the lid on and cook on high for 3 hours or until the rice and vegetables are tender.
6. Pour them in a large serving bowl, then spread with Parmesan cheese before serving.

Per Serving

calories: 499 | fat: 16.4g | protein: 32.4g | carbs: 56.5g | fiber: 4.7g | sodium: 758mg

Papaya, Jicama, and Peas Rice Bowl

Prep time: 20 minutes | Cook time: 45 minutes | Serves 4

Sauce:
Juice of ¼ lemon
2 teaspoons chopped fresh basil
1 tablespoon raw honey
1 tablespoon extra-virgin olive oil
Sea salt, to taste

Rice:
1½ cups wild rice
2 papayas, peeled, seeded, and diced
1 jicama, peeled and shredded
1 cup snow peas, julienned
2 cups shredded cabbage
1 scallion, white and green parts, chopped

1. Combine the ingredients for the sauce in a bowl. Stir to mix well. Set aside until ready to use.
2. Pour the wild rice in a saucepan, then pour in enough water to cover. Bring to a boil.
3. Reduce the heat to low, then simmer for 45 minutes or until the wild rice is soft and plump. Drain and transfer to a large serving bowl.
4. Top the rice with papayas, jicama, peas, cabbage, and scallion. Pour the sauce over and stir to mix well before serving.

Per Serving

calories: 446 | fat: 7.9g | protein: 13.1g | carbs: 85.8g | fiber: 16.0g | sodium: 70mg

Black Bean Chili with Mangoes

Prep time: 10 minutes | Cook time: 10 minutes | Serves 4

2 tablespoons coconut oil
1 onion, chopped
2 (15-ounce / 425-g) cans black beans, drained and rinsed
1 tablespoon chili powder
1 teaspoon sea salt
¼ teaspoon freshly ground black pepper
1 cup water
2 ripe mangoes, sliced thinly
¼ cup chopped fresh cilantro, divided
¼ cup sliced scallions, divided

1. Heat the coconut oil in a pot over high heat until melted.
2. Put the onion in the pot and sauté for 5 minutes or until translucent. Add the black beans to the pot. Sprinkle with chili powder, salt, and ground black pepper. Pour in the water. Stir to mix well.
3. Bring to a boil. Reduce the heat to low, then simmering for 5 minutes or until the beans are tender.
4. Turn off the heat and mix in the mangoes, then garnish with scallions and cilantro before serving.

Per Serving

calories: 430 | fat: 9.1g | protein: 20.2g | carbs: 71.9g | fiber: 22.0g | sodium: 608mg

Vegetable Mains

Cheesy Sweet Potato Burgers

Prep time: 10 minutes | Cook time: 19 to 20 minutes | Serves 4

1 large sweet potato (about 8 ounces / 227 g)	1 garlic clove
2 tablespoons extra-virgin olive oil, divided	1 cup old-fashioned rolled oats
1 cup chopped onion	1 tablespoon dried oregano
1 large egg	1 tablespoon balsamic vinegar
	¼ teaspoon kosher salt
	½ cup crumbled Gorgonzola cheese

1. Using a fork, pierce the sweet potato all over and microwave on high for 4 to 5 minutes, until softened in the center. Cool slightly before slicing in half.
2. Meanwhile, in a large skillet over medium-high heat, heat 1 tablespoon of the olive oil. Add the onion and sauté for 5 minutes.
3. Spoon the sweet potato flesh out of the skin and put the flesh in a food processor. Add the cooked onion, egg, garlic, oats, oregano, vinegar and salt. Pulse until smooth. Add the cheese and pulse four times to barely combine.
4. Form the mixture into four burgers. Place the burgers on a plate, and press to flatten each to about ¾-inch thick.
5. Wipe out the skillet with a paper towel. Heat the remaining 1 tablespoon of the oil over medium-high heat for about 2 minutes. Add the burgers to the hot oil, then reduce the heat to medium. Cook the burgers for 5 minutes per side.
6. Transfer the burgers to a plate and serve.

Per Serving

calories: 290 | fat: 12.0g | protein: 12.0g | carbs: 43.0g | fiber: 8.0g | sodium: 566mg

Veggie-Stuffed Portabello Mushrooms

Prep time: 5 minutes | Cook time: 24 to 25 minutes | Serves 6

3 tablespoons extra-virgin olive oil, divided	¼ teaspoon kosher salt
1 cup diced onion	¼ teaspoon crushed red pepper
2 garlic cloves, minced	6 large portabello mushrooms, stems and gills removed
1 large zucchini, diced	
3 cups chopped mushrooms	
1 cup chopped tomato	Cooking spray
1 teaspoon dried oregano	4 ounces (113 g) fresh Mozzarella cheese, shredded

1. In a large skillet over medium heat, heat 2 tablespoons of the oil. Add the onion and sauté for 4 minutes. Stir in the garlic and sauté for 1 minute.
2. Stir in the zucchini, mushrooms, tomato, oregano, salt and red pepper. Cook for 10 minutes, stirring constantly. Remove from the heat.
3. Meanwhile, heat a grill pan over medium-high heat.
4. Brush the remaining 1 tablespoon of the oil over the portabello mushroom caps. Place the mushrooms, bottom-side down, on the grill pan. Cover with a sheet of aluminum foil sprayed with nonstick cooking spray. Cook for 5 minutes.
5. Flip the mushroom caps over, and spoon about ½ cup of the cooked vegetable mixture into each cap. Top each with about 2½ tablespoons of the Mozzarella.
6. Cover and grill for 4 to 5 minutes, or until the cheese is melted.
7. Using a spatula, transfer the portabello mushrooms to a plate. Let cool for about 5 minutes before serving.

Per Serving

calories: 111 | fat: 4.0g | protein: 11.0g | carbs: 11.0g | fiber: 4.0g | sodium: 314mg

Chickpea Lettuce Wraps with Celery

Prep time: 10 minutes | Cook time: 0 minutes | Serves 4

1 (15-ounce / 425-g) can low-sodium chickpeas, drained and rinsed
1 celery stalk, thinly sliced
2 tablespoons finely chopped red onion
2 tablespoons unsalted tahini
3 tablespoons honey mustard
1 tablespoon capers, undrained
12 butter lettuce leaves

1. In a bowl, mash the chickpeas with a potato masher or the back of a fork until mostly smooth.
2. Add the celery, red onion, tahini, honey mustard, and capers to the bowl and stir until well incorporated.
3. For each serving, place three overlapping lettuce leaves on a plate and top with ¼ of the mashed chickpea filling, then roll up. Repeat with the remaining lettuce leaves and chickpea mixture.

Per Serving

calories: 182 | fat: 7.1g | protein: 10.3g | carbs: 19.6g | fiber: 3.0g | sodium: 171mg

Honey-Glazed Baby Carrots

Prep time: 5 minutes | Cook time: 6 minutes | Serves 2

⅔ cup water
1½ pounds (680 g) baby carrots
4 tablespoons almond butter
½ cup honey
1 teaspoon dried thyme
1½ teaspoons dried dill Salt, to taste

1. Pour the water into the Instant Pot and add a steamer basket. Place the baby carrots in the basket.
2. Secure the lid. Select the Manual mode and set the cooking time for 4 minutes at High Pressure.
3. Once cooking is complete, do a quick pressure release. Carefully open the lid.
4. Transfer the carrots to a plate and set aside.
5. Pour the water out of the Instant Pot and dry it.
6. Press the Sauté button on the Instant Pot and heat the almond butter.
7. Stir in the honey, thyme, and dill.
8. Return the carrots to the Instant Pot and stir until well coated. Sauté for another 1 minute.
9. Taste and season with salt as needed. Serve warm.

Per Serving

calories: 575 | fat: 23.5g | protein: 2.8g | carbs: 90.6g | fiber: 10.3g | sodium: 547mg

Quick Steamed Broccoli

Prep time: 5 minutes | Cook time: 0 minutes | Serves 2

¼ cup water
3 cups broccoli florets
Salt and ground black pepper, to taste

1. Pour the water into the Instant Pot and insert a steamer basket. Place the broccoli florets in the basket.
2. Secure the lid. Select the Manual mode and set the cooking time for 0 minutes at High Pressure.
3. Once cooking is complete, do a quick pressure release. Carefully open the lid.
4. Transfer the broccoli florets to a bowl with cold water to keep bright green color.
5. Season the broccoli with salt and pepper to taste, then serve.

Per Serving

calories: 16 | fat: 0.2g | protein: 1.9g | carbs: 1.7g | fiber: 1.6g | sodium: 292mg

Garlic-Butter Asparagus with Parmesan

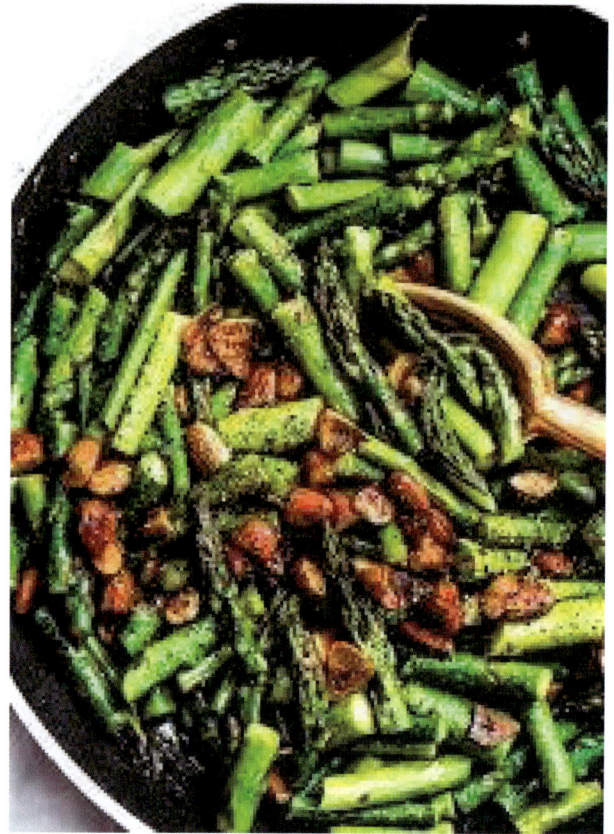

Prep time: 5 minutes | Cook time: 8 minutes | Serves 2

1 cup water
1 pound (454 g) asparagus, trimmed
2 cloves garlic, chopped
3 tablespoons almond butter
Salt and ground black pepper, to taste
3 tablespoons grated Parmesan cheese

1. Pour the water into the Instant Pot and insert a trivet.
2. Put the asparagus on a tin foil add the butter and garlic. Season to taste with salt and pepper.
3. Fold over the foil and seal the asparagus inside so the foil doesn't come open. Arrange the asparagus on the trivet.
4. Secure the lid. Select the Manual mode and set the cooking time for 8 minutes at High Pressure.
5. Once cooking is complete, do a quick pressure release. Carefully open the lid. Unwrap the foil packet and serve sprinkled with the Parmesan cheese.

Per Serving

calories: 243 | fat: 15.7g | protein: 12.3g | carbs: 15.3g | fiber: 7.3g | sodium: 435mg

Ratatouille

Prep time: 10 minutes | Cook time: 6 minutes | Serves 4

2 large zucchinis, sliced	2 teaspoons sea salt
2 medium eggplants, sliced	1 teaspoon black pepper
4 medium tomatoes, sliced	2 tablespoons balsamic
2 small red onions, sliced	vinegar
4 cloves garlic, chopped	4 tablespoons olive oil
2 tablespoons thyme leaves	2 cups water

1. Line a springform pan with foil and place the chopped garlic in the bottom.
2. Now arrange the vegetable slices, alternately, in circles.
3. Sprinkle the thyme, pepper and salt over the vegetables. Top with oil and vinegar.
4. Pour a cup of water into the instant pot and place the trivet inside. Secure the lid and cook on Manual function for 6 minutes at High Pressure.
5. Release the pressure naturally and remove the lid.
6. Remove the vegetables along with the tin foil.
7. Serve on a platter and enjoy.

Per Serving

calories: 240 | fat: 14.3g | protein: 4.7g | carbs: 27.5g | fiber: 10.8g | sodium: 1181mg

Mushroom and Potato Teriyaki

Prep time: 10 minutes | Cook time: 18 minutes | Serves 4

¾ large yellow or white onion, chopped	¼ cup tomato paste
1½ medium carrots, diced	½ tablespoon sesame oil
1½ ribs celery, chopped	2 teaspoons sesame seeds
1 medium portabella mushroom, diced	½ tablespoon paprika
¾ tablespoon garlic, chopped	1 teaspoon fresh rosemary
2 cups water	¾ cups peas
1 pound (454 g) white potatoes, peeled and diced	¼ cup fresh parsley for garnishing, chopped

1. Add the oil, sesame seeds, and all the vegetables in the instant pot and Sauté for 5 minutes.
2. Stir in the remaining ingredients and secure the lid.
3. Cook on Manual function for 13 minutes at High Pressure.
4. After the beep, natural release the pressure and remove the lid.
5. Garnish with fresh parsley and serve hot.

Per Serving

calories: 160 | fat: 3.0g | protein: 4.7g | carbs: 30.6g | fiber: 5.5g | sodium: 52mg

Cauliflower with Sweet Potato

Prep time: 15 minutes | Cook time: 8 minutes | Serves 8

1 small onion
4 tomatoes
4 garlic cloves, chopped
2-inch ginger, chopped
2 teaspoons olive oil
1 teaspoon turmeric
2 teaspoons ground cumin
Salt, to taste

1 teaspoon paprika
2 medium sweet potatoes, cubed small
2 small cauliflowers, diced
2 tablespoons fresh cilantro for topping, chopped

1. Blend the tomatoes, garlic, ginger and onion in a blender.
2. Add the oil and cumin in the instant pot and Sauté for 1 minute.
3. Stir in the blended mixture and the remaining spices.
4. Add the sweet potatoes and cook for 5 minutes on Sauté
5. Add the cauliflower chunks and secure the lid.
6. Cook on Manual for 2 minutes at High Pressure.
7. Once done, Quick release the pressure and remove the lid.
8. Stir and serve with cilantro on top.

Per Serving

calories: 76 | fat: 1.6g | protein: 2.7g | carbs: 14.4g | fiber: 3.4g | sodium: 55mg

Potato Curry

Prep time: 10 minutes | Cook time: 30 minutes | Serves 2

2 large potatoes, peeled and diced
1 small onion, peeled and diced
8 ounces (227 g) fresh tomatoes
1 tablespoon olive oil
1 cup water

2 tablespoons garlic cloves, grated
½ tablespoon rosemary
½ tablespoon cayenne pepper
1½ tablespoons thyme
Salt and pepper, to taste

1. Pour a cup of water into the instant pot and place the steamer trivet inside.
2. Place the potatoes and half the garlic over the trivet and sprinkle some salt and pepper on top.
3. Secure the lid and cook on Steam function for 20 minutes.
4. After the beep, natural release the pressure and remove the lid.
5. Put the potatoes to one side and empty the pot.
6. Add the remaining ingredients to the cooker and Sauté for 10 minutes.
7. Use an immerse blender to purée the cooked mixture.
8. Stir in the steamed potatoes and serve hot.

Per Serving

calories: 398 | fat: 7.6g | protein: 9.6g | carbs: 76.2g | fiber: 10.9g | sodium: 111mg

Poultry and Meats

Prep time: 10 minutes | Cook time: 15 minutes | Serves 4

3 tablespoons fresh rosemary leaves
¼ cup Dijon mustard
½ cup fresh parsley leaves
6 garlic cloves
½ teaspoon sea salt
¼ teaspoon freshly ground black pepper
1 tablespoon extra-virgin olive oil
1 (1½-pound / 680-g) pork tenderloin

1. Preheat the oven to 400ºF (205ºC).
2. Put all the ingredients, except for the pork tenderloin, in a food processor. Pulse until it has a thick consistency.
3. Put the pork tenderloin on a baking sheet, then rub with the mixture to coat well.
4. Put the sheet in the preheated oven and bake for 15 minutes or until the internal temperature of the pork reaches at least 165ºF (74ºC). Flip the tenderloin halfway through the cooking time.
5. Transfer the cooked pork tenderloin to a large plate and allow to cool for 5 minutes before serving.

Per Serving

calories: 363 | fat: 18.1g | protein: 2.2g | carbs: 4.9g | fiber: 2.0g | sodium: 514mg

Macadamia Pork

Prep time: 10 minutes | Cook time: 10 minutes | Serves 4

1 (1-pound / 454-g) pork tenderloin, cut into ½-inch slices and pounded thin
1 teaspoon sea salt, divided
¼ teaspoon freshly ground black pepper, divided
½ cup macadamia nuts
1 cup unsweetened coconut milk
1 tablespoon extra-virgin olive oil

1. Preheat the oven to 400ºF (205ºC).
2. On a clean work surface, rub the pork with ½ teaspoon of the salt and ⅛ teaspoon of the ground black pepper. Set aside. Ground the macadamia nuts in a food processor, then combine with remaining salt and black pepper in a bowl. Stir to mix well and set aside.
3. Combine the coconut milk and olive oil in a separate bowl. Stir to mix well.
4. Dredge the pork chops into the bowl of coconut milk mixture, then dunk into the bowl of macadamia nut mixture to coat well. Shake the excess off.
5. Put the well-coated pork chops on a baking sheet, then bake for 10 minutes or until the internal temperature of the pork reaches at least 165ºF (74ºC).
6. Transfer the pork chops to a serving plate and serve immediately.

Per Serving

calories: 436 | fat: 32.8g | protein: 33.1g | carbs: 5.9g | fiber: 3.0g | sodium: 310mg

Grilled Chicken and Zucchini Kebabs

Prep time: 10 minutes | Cook time: 20 minutes | Serves 4

¼ cup extra-virgin olive oil
2 tablespoons balsamic vinegar
1 teaspoon dried oregano, crushed between your fingers
1 pound (454 g) boneless, skinless chicken breasts, cut into 1½-inch pieces
2 medium zucchinis, cut into 1-inch pieces
½ cup Kalamata olives, pitted and halved
2 tablespoons olive brine
¼ cup torn fresh basil leaves
Nonstick cooking spray

Special Equipment:

14 to 15 (12-inch) wooden skewers, soaked for at least 30 minutes

1. Spray the grill grates with nonstick cooking spray. Preheat the grill to medium-high heat.
2. In a small bowl, whisk together the olive oil, vinegar, and oregano. Divide the marinade between two large plastic zip-top bags.
3. Add the chicken to one bag and the zucchini to another. Seal and massage the marinade into both the chicken and zucchini.
4. Thread the chicken onto 6 wooden skewers. Thread the zucchini onto 8 or 9 wooden skewers.
5. Cook the kebabs in batches on the grill for 5 minutes, flip, and grill for 5 minutes more, or until any chicken juices run clear.
6. Remove the chicken and zucchini from the skewers to a large serving bowl. Toss with the olives, olive brine, and basil and serve.

Per Serving

calories: 283 | fat: 15.0g | protein: 11.0g | carbs: 26.0g | fiber: 3.0g | sodium: 575mg

Beef Kebabs with Onion and Pepper

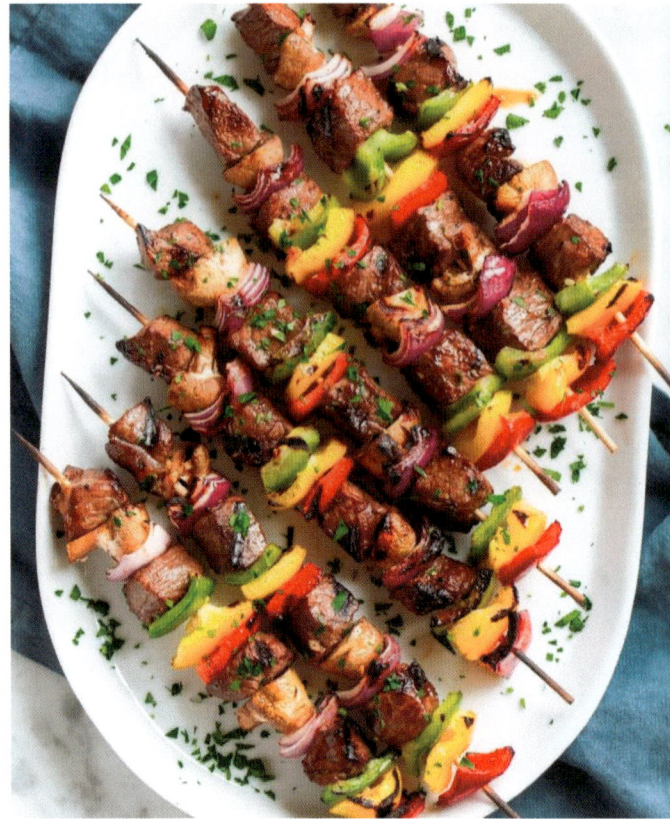

Prep time: 15 minutes | Cook time: 10 minutes | Serves 6

2 pounds (907 g) beef fillet
1½ teaspoons salt
1 teaspoon freshly ground black pepper
½ teaspoon ground nutmeg
½ teaspoon ground allspice
⅓ cup extra-virgin olive oil
1 large onion, cut into 8 quarters
1 large red bell pepper, cut into 1-inch cubes

1. Preheat the grill to high heat.
2. Cut the beef into 1-inch cubes and put them in a large bowl.
3. In a small bowl, mix together the salt, black pepper, allspice, and nutmeg.
4. Pour the olive oil over the beef and toss to coat. Evenly sprinkle the seasoning over the beef and toss to coat all pieces.
5. Skewer the beef, alternating every 1 or 2 pieces with a piece of onion or bell pepper.
6. To cook, place the skewers on the preheated grill, and flip every 2 to 3 minutes until all sides have cooked to desired doneness, 6 minutes for medium-rare, 8 minutes for well done. Serve hot.

Per Serving

calories: 485 | fat: 36.0g | protein: 35.0g | carbs: 4.0g | fiber: 1.0g | sodium: 1453mg

Grilled Pork Chops

Prep time: 20 minutes | Cook time: 10 minutes | Serves 4

¼ cup extra-virgin olive oil
2 tablespoons fresh thyme leaves
1 teaspoon smoked paprika
1 teaspoon salt
4 pork loin chops, ½-inch-thick

1. In a small bowl, mix together the olive oil, thyme, paprika, and salt. Put the pork chops in a plastic zip-top bag or a bowl and coat them with the spice mix. Let them marinate for 15 minutes.
2. Preheat the grill to high heat. Cook the pork chops for 4 minutes on each side until cooked through. Serve warm.

Per Serving

calories: 282 | fat: 23.0g | protein: 21.0g | carbs: 1.0g | fiber: 0g | sodium: 832mg

Greek-Style Lamb Burgers

Prep time: 10 minutes | Cook time: 10 minutes | Serves 4

1 pound (454 g) ground lamb
½ teaspoon salt
½ teaspoon freshly ground black pepper
4 tablespoons crumbled feta cheese
Buns, toppings, and tzatziki, for serving (optional)

1. Preheat the grill to high heat. In a large bowl, using your hands, combine the lamb with the salt and pepper.
2. Divide the meat into 4 portions. Divide each portion in half to make a top and a bottom. Flatten each half into a 3-inch circle. Make a dent in the center of one of the halves and place 1 tablespoon of the feta cheese in the center. Place the second half of the patty on top of the feta cheese and press down to close the 2 halves together, making it resemble a round burger. Grill each side for 3 minutes, for medium-well. Serve on a bun with your favorite toppings and tzatziki sauce, if desired.

Per Serving

calories: 345 | fat: 29.0g | protein: 20.0g | carbs: 1.0g | fiber: 0g | sodium: 462mg

Chicken Bruschetta Burgers

Prep time: 10 minutes | Cook time: 16 minutes | Serves 2

1 tablespoon olive oil
2 garlic cloves, minced
3 tablespoons finely minced onion
1 teaspoon dried basil
3 tablespoons minced sun-dried tomatoes packed in olive oil
8 ounces (227 g) ground chicken breast
¼ teaspoon salt
3 pieces small Mozzarella balls, minced

1. Heat the olive oil in a nonstick skillet over medium-high heat. Add the garlic and onion and sauté for 5 minutes until tender. Stir in the basil. Remove from the skillet to a medium bowl. Add the tomatoes, ground chicken, and salt and stir until incorporated. Mix in the Mozzarella balls.
2. Divide the chicken mixture in half and form into two burgers, each about ¾-inch thick.
3. Heat the same skillet over medium-high heat and add the burgers. Cook each side for 5 to 6 minutes, or until they reach an internal temperature of 165ºF (74ºC).
4. Serve warm.

Per Serving

calories: 300 | fat: 17.0g | protein: 32.2g | carbs: 6.0g | fiber: 1.1g | sodium: 724mg

Chicken Cacciatore

Prep time: 15 minutes | Cook time: 1 hour and 30 minutes | Serves 2

1½ pounds (680 g) bone-in chicken thighs, skin removed and patted dry
Salt, to taste
2 tablespoons olive oil
½ large onion, thinly sliced
4 ounces (113 g) baby bella mushrooms, sliced
1 red sweet pepper, cut into 1-inch pieces
1 (15-ounce / 425-g) can crushed fire-roasted tomatoes
1 fresh rosemary sprig
½ cup dry red wine
1 teaspoon Italian herb seasoning
½ teaspoon garlic powder
3 tablespoons flour

1. Season the chicken thighs with a generous pinch of salt.
2. Heat the olive oil in a Dutch oven over medium-high heat. Add the chicken and brown for 5 minutes per side.
3. Add the onion, mushrooms, and sweet pepper to the Dutch oven and sauté for another 5 minutes.
4. Add the tomatoes, rosemary, wine, Italian seasoning, garlic powder, and salt, stirring well.
5. Bring the mixture to a boil, then reduce the heat to low. Allow to simmer slowly for at least 1 hour, stirring occasionally, or until the chicken is tender and easily pulls away from the bone.
6. Measure out 1 cup of the sauce from the pot and put it into a bowl. Add the flour and whisk well to make a slurry.
7. Increase the heat to medium-high and slowly whisk the slurry into the pot. Stir until it comes to a boil and cook until the sauce is thickened.
8. Remove the chicken from the bones and shred it, and add it back to the sauce before serving, if desired.

Per Serving

calories: 520 | fat: 23.1g | protein: 31.8g | carbs: 37.0g | fiber: 6.0g | sodium: 484mg

Spiced Roast Chicken

Prep time: 10 minutes | Cook time: 35 minutes | Serves 6

1 teaspoon garlic powder	½ teaspoon salt
1 teaspoon ground paprika	¼ teaspoon ground cayenne
½ teaspoon ground cumin	pepper
½ teaspoon ground coriander	6 chicken legs
	1 teaspoon extra-virgin olive oil

1. Preheat the oven to 400ºF (205ºC).
2. Combine the garlic powder, paprika, cumin, coriander, salt, and cayenne pepper in a small bowl.
3. On a clean work surface, rub the spices all over the chicken legs until completely coated.
4. Heat the olive oil in an ovenproof skillet over medium heat.
5. Add the chicken thighs and sear each side for 8 to 10 minutes, or until the skin is crispy and browned.
6. Transfer the skillet to the preheated oven and continue cooking for 10 to 15 minutes, or until the juices run clear and it registers an internal temperature of 165ºF (74ºC).
7. Remove from the heat and serve on plates.

Per Serving

calories: 275 | fat: 15.6g | protein: 30.3g | carbs: 0.9g | fiber: 0g | sodium: 255mg

Yogurt Chicken Breasts

Prep time: 10 minutes | Cook time: 10 minutes | Serves 4

1 pound (454 g) boneless, skinless chicken breasts, cut into 2-inch strips	Pinch saffron (3 or 4 threads)
1 tablespoon extra-virgin olive oil	3 garlic cloves, minced
	½ onion, chopped
Yogurt Sauce:	2 tablespoons chopped fresh cilantro
½ cup plain Greek yogurt	Juice of ½ lemon
2 tablespoons water	½ teaspoon salt

1. Make the yogurt sauce: Place the yogurt, water, saffron, garlic, onion, cilantro, lemon juice, and salt in a blender, and pulse until completely mixed.
2. Transfer the yogurt sauce to a large bowl, along with the chicken strips. Toss to coat well.
3. Cover with plastic wrap and marinate in the refrigerator for at least 1 hour, or up to overnight.
4. When ready to cook, heat the olive oil in a large skillet over medium heat.
5. Add the chicken strips to the skillet, discarding any excess marinade. Cook each side for 5 minutes, or until cooked through.
6. Let the chicken cool for 5 minutes before serving.

Per Serving

calories: 154 | fat: 4.8g | protein: 26.3g | carbs: 2.9g | fiber: 0g | sodium: 500mg

Fish and Seafood

Cioppino (Seafood Tomato Stew)

Prep time: 10 minutes | Cook time: 20 minutes | Serves 2

2 tablespoons olive oil
½ small onion, diced
½ green pepper, diced
2 teaspoons dried basil
2 teaspoons dried oregano
½ cup dry white wine
1 (14.5-ounce / 411-g) can diced tomatoes with basil
1 (8-ounce / 227-g) can no-salt-added tomato sauce

1 (6.5-ounce / 184-g) can minced clams with their juice
8 ounces (227 g) peeled, deveined raw shrimp
4 ounces (113 g) any white fish (a thick piece works best)
3 tablespoons fresh parsley
Salt and freshly ground black pepper, to taste

1. In a Dutch oven, heat the olive oil over medium heat.
2. Sauté the onion and green pepper for 5 minutes, or until tender. Stir in the basil, oregano, wine, diced tomatoes, and tomato sauce and bring to a boil.
3. Once boiling, reduce the heat to low and bring to a simmer for 5 minutes.
4. Add the clams, shrimp, and fish and cook for about 10 minutes, or until the shrimp are pink and cooked through.
5. Scatter with the parsley and add the salt and black pepper to taste. Remove from the heat and serve warm.

Per Serving

calories: 221 | fat: 7.7g | protein: 23.1g | carbs: 10.9g | fiber: 4.2g | sodium: 720mg

Lemon Grilled Shrimp

Prep time: 20 minutes | Cook time: 4 to 6 minutes | Serves 4

2 tablespoons garlic, minced
3 tablespoons fresh Italian parsley, finely chopped
¼ cup extra-virgin olive oil
½ cup lemon juice

1 teaspoon salt
2 pounds (907 g) jumbo shrimp (21 to 25), peeled and deveined
Special Equipment:
4 wooden skewers, soaked in water for at least 30 minutes

1. Whisk together the garlic, parsley, olive oil, lemon juice, and salt in a large bowl.
2. Add the shrimp to the bowl and toss well, making sure the shrimp are coated in the marinade. Set aside to sit for 15 minutes.
3. When ready, skewer the shrimps by piercing through the center. You can place about 5 to 6 shrimps on each skewer.
4. Preheat the grill to high heat.
5. Grill the shrimp for 4 to 6 minutes, flipping the shrimp halfway through, or until the shrimp are pink on the outside and opaque in the center. Serve hot.

Per Serving

calories: 401 | fat: 17.8g | protein: 56.9g | carbs: 3.9g | fiber: 0g | sodium: 1223mg

Garlic Shrimp with Mushrooms

Prep time: 10 minutes | Cook time: 15 minutes | Serves 4

1 pound (454 g) fresh shrimp, peeled, deveined, and patted dry
1 teaspoon salt
1 cup extra-virgin olive oil
8 large garlic cloves, thinly sliced

4 ounces (113 g) sliced mushrooms (shiitake, baby bella, or button)
½ teaspoon red pepper flakes
¼ cup chopped fresh flat-leaf Italian parsley

1. In a bowl, season the shrimp with salt. Set aside.
2. Heat the olive oil in a large skillet over medium-low heat.
3. Add the garlic and cook for 3 to 4 minutes until fragrant, stirring occasionally.
4. Sauté the mushrooms for 5 minutes, or until they start to exude their juices. Stir in the shrimp and sprinkle with red pepper flakes and sauté for 3 to 4 minutes more, or until the shrimp start to turn pink.
5. Remove the skillet from the heat and add the parsley. Stir to combine and serve warm.

Per Serving

calories: 619 | fat: 55.5g | protein: 24.1g | carbs: 3.7g | fiber: 0g | sodium: 735mg

Lemony Shrimp with Orzo Salad

Prep time: 10 minutes | Cook time: 22 minutes | Serves 4

1 cup orzo
1 hothouse cucumber, deseeded and chopped
½ cup finely diced red onion
2 tablespoons extra-virgin olive oil
2 pounds (907 g) shrimp, peeled and deveined

3 lemons, juiced
Salt and freshly ground black pepper, to taste
¾ cup crumbled feta cheese
2 tablespoons dried dill
1 cup chopped fresh flat-leaf parsley

1. Bring a large pot of water to a boil. Add the orzo and cook covered for 15 to 18 minutes, or until the orzo is tender. Transfer to a colander to drain and set aside to cool.
2. Mix the cucumber and red onion in a bowl. Set aside.
3. Heat the olive oil in a medium skillet over medium heat until it shimmers.
4. Reduce the heat, add the shrimp, and cook each side for 2 minutes until cooked through.
5. Add the cooked shrimp to the bowl of cucumber and red onion. Mix in the cooked orzo and lemon juice and toss to combine. Sprinkle with salt and pepper. Scatter the top with the feta cheese and dill. Garnish with the parsley and serve immediately.

Per Serving

calories: 565 | fat: 17.8g | protein: 63.3g | carbs: 43.9g | fiber: 4.1g | sodium: 2225mg

Avocado Shrimp Ceviche

Prep time: 15 minutes | Cook time: 0 minutes | Serves 4

1 pound (454 g) fresh shrimp, peeled, deveined, and cut in half lengthwise
1 small red or yellow bell pepper, cut into ½-inch chunks
½ small red onion, cut into thin slivers
½ English cucumber, peeled and cut into ½-inch chunks
¼ cup chopped fresh cilantro
½ cup extra-virgin olive oil
⅓ cup freshly squeezed lime juice
2 tablespoons freshly squeezed clementine juice
2 tablespoons freshly squeezed lemon juice
1 teaspoon salt
½ teaspoon freshly ground black pepper
2 ripe avocados, peeled, pitted, and cut into ½-inch chunks

1. Place the shrimp, bell pepper, red onion, cucumber, and cilantro in a large bowl and toss to combine.
2. In a separate bowl, stir together the olive oil, lime, clementine, and lemon juice, salt, and black pepper until smooth. Pour the mixture into the bowl of shrimp and vegetable mixture and toss until they are completely coated.
3. Cover the bowl with plastic wrap and transfer to the refrigerator to marinate for at least 2 hours, or up to 8 hours.
4. When ready, stir in the avocado chunks and toss to incorporate. Serve immediately.

Per Serving

calories: 496 | fat: 39.5g | protein: 25.3g | carbs: 13.8g | fiber: 6.0g | sodium: 755mg

Spicy Grilled Shrimp with Lemon Wedges

Prep time: 15 minutes | Cook time: 6 minutes | Serves 6

1 large clove garlic, crushed
1 teaspoon coarse salt
1 teaspoon paprika
½ teaspoon cayenne pepper
2 teaspoons lemon juice
2 tablespoons plus 1 teaspoon olive oil, divided
2 pounds (907 g) large shrimp, peeled and deveined
8 wedges lemon, for garnish

1. Preheat the grill to medium heat.
2. Stir together the garlic, salt, paprika, cayenne pepper, lemon juice, and 2 tablespoons of olive oil in a small bowl until a paste forms. Add the shrimp and toss until well coated.
3. Grease the grill grates lightly with remaining 1 teaspoon of olive oil.
4. Grill the shrimp for 4 to 6 minutes, flipping the shrimp halfway through, or until the shrimp is totally pink and opaque.
5. Garnish the shrimp with lemon wedges and serve hot.

Per Serving

calories: 163 | fat: 5.8g | protein: 25.2g | carbs: 2.8g | fiber: 0.4g | sodium: 585mg

Cod with Parsley Pistou

Prep time: 15 minutes | Cook time: 10 minutes | Serves 4

1 cup packed roughly chopped fresh flat-leaf Italian parsley
Zest and juice of 1 lemon
1 to 2 small garlic cloves, minced
1 teaspoon salt
½ teaspoon freshly ground black pepper
1 cup extra-virgin olive oil, divided
1 pound (454 g) cod fillets, cut into 4 equal-sized pieces

1. Make the pistou: Place the parsley, lemon zest and juice, garlic, salt, and pepper in a food processor until finely chopped. With the food processor running, slowly drizzle in ¾ cup of olive oil until a thick sauce forms. Set aside.
2. Heat the remaining ¼ cup of olive oil in a large skillet over medium-high heat.
3. Add the cod fillets, cover, and cook each side for 4 to 5 minutes, until browned and cooked through.
4. Remove the cod fillets from the heat to a plate and top each with generous spoonfuls of the prepared pistou. Serve immediately.

Per Serving

calories: 580 | fat: 54.6g | protein: 21.1g | carbs: 2.8g | fiber: 1.0g | sodium: 651mg

Fried Cod Fillets

Prep time: 5 minutes | Cook time: 10 minutes | Serves 4

½ cup all-purpose flour
1 teaspoon garlic powder
1 teaspoon salt
4 (4- to 5-ounce / 113- to 142-g) cod fillets
1 tablespoon extra-virgin olive oil

1. Mix together the flour, garlic powder, and salt in a shallow dish. Dredge each piece of fish in the seasoned flour until they are evenly coated.
2. Heat the olive oil in a medium skillet over medium-high heat. Once hot, add the cod fillets and fry for 6 to 8 minutes, flipping the fish halfway through, or until the fish is opaque and flakes easily.
3. Remove from the heat and serve on plates.

Per Serving

calories: 333 | fat: 18.8g | protein: 21.2g | carbs: 20.0g | fiber: 5.7g | sodium: 870mg

Mediterranean Braised Cod with Vegetables

Prep time: 10 minutes | Cook time: 18 minutes | Serves 2

1 tablespoon olive oil
½ medium onion, minced
2 garlic cloves, minced
1 teaspoon oregano
1 (15-ounce / 425-g) can artichoke hearts in water, drained and halved
1 (15-ounce / 425-g) can diced tomatoes with basil
¼ cup pitted Greek olives, drained
10 ounces (284 g) wild cod
Salt and freshly ground black pepper, to taste

1. In a skillet, heat the olive oil over medium-high heat.
2. Sauté the onion for about 5 minutes, stirring occasionally, or until tender. Stir in the garlic and oregano and cook for 30 seconds more until fragrant.
3. Add the artichoke hearts, tomatoes, and olives and stir to combine. Top with the cod. Cover and cook for 10 minutes, or until the fish flakes easily with a fork and juices run clean. Sprinkle with the salt and pepper. Serve warm.

Per Serving

calories: 332 | fat: 10.5g | protein: 29.2g | carbs: 30.7g | fiber: 8.0g | sodium: 1906mg

Lemon-Parsley Swordfish

Prep time: 10 minutes | Cook time: 17 to 20 minutes | Serves 4

1 cup fresh Italian parsley
¼ cup lemon juice
¼ cup extra-virgin olive oil
¼ cup fresh thyme
2 cloves garlic
½ teaspoon salt
4 swordfish steaks
Olive oil spray

1. Preheat the oven to 450ºF (235ºC). Grease a large baking dish generously with olive oil spray.
2. Place the parsley, lemon juice, olive oil, thyme, garlic, and salt in a food processor and pulse until smoothly blended.
3. Arrange the swordfish steaks in the greased baking dish and spoon the parsley mixture over the top.
4. Bake in the preheated oven for 17 to 20 minutes until flaky.
5. Divide the fish among four plates and serve hot.

Per Serving

calories: 396 | fat: 21.7g | protein: 44.2g | carbs: 2.9g | fiber: 1.0g | sodium: 494mg

Fruits and Desserts

Watermelon and Blueberry Salad

Prep time: 5 minutes | Cook time: 0 minutes | Serves 6 to 8

1 medium watermelon
1 cup fresh blueberries
⅓ cup honey

2 tablespoons lemon juice
2 tablespoons finely chopped
fresh mint leaves

1. Cut the watermelon into 1-inch cubes. Put them in a bowl.
2. Evenly distribute the blueberries over the watermelon.
3. In a separate bowl, whisk together the honey, lemon juice and mint. Drizzle the mint dressing over the watermelon and blueberries. Serve cold.

Per Serving

calories: 238 | fat: 1.0g | protein: 4.0g | carbs: 61.0g | fiber: 3.0g | sodium: 11mg

Crispy Sesame Cookies

Prep time: 5 minutes | Cook time: 8 to 10 minutes | Serves 14 to 16

1 cup hulled sesame seeds
1 cup sugar

8 tablespoons almond butter
2 large eggs
1¼ cups flour

1. Preheat the oven to 350ºF (180ºC).
2. Toast the sesame seeds on a baking sheet for 3 minutes. Set aside and let cool. Using a mixer, whisk together the sugar and butter. Add the eggs one at a time until well blended. Add the flour and toasted sesame seeds and mix until well blended. Drop spoonfuls of cookie dough onto a baking sheet and form them into round balls, about 1-inch in diameter, similar to a walnut.
3. Put in the oven and bake for 5 to 7 minutes, or until golden brown. Let the cookies cool for 5 minutes before serving.

Per Serving

calories: 218 | fat: 12.0g | protein: 4.0g | carbs: 25.0g | fiber: 2.0g | sodium: 58mg

Mint Banana Chocolate Sorbet

Prep time: 4 hours 5 minutes | Cook time: 0 minutes | Serves 1

1 frozen banana
1 tablespoon almond butter
2 tablespoons minced fresh mint

2 to 3 tablespoons dark chocolate chips (60% cocoa or higher)
2 to 3 tablespoons goji (optional)

1. Put the banana, butter, and mint in a food processor. Pulse to purée until creamy and smooth.
2. Add the chocolate and goji, then pulse for several more times to combine well. Pour the mixture in a bowl or a ramekin, then freeze for at least 4 hours before serving chilled.

Per Serving

calories: 213 | fat: 9.8g | protein: 3.1g | carbs: 2.9g | fiber: 4.0g | sodium: 155mg

Pecan and Carrot Cake

Prep time: 15 minutes | Cook time: 45 minutes | Serves 12

½ cup coconut oil, at room temperature, plus more for greasing the baking dish
2 teaspoons pure vanilla extract
¼ cup pure maple syrup 6 eggs
½ cup coconut flour
1 teaspoon baking powder

1 teaspoon baking soda
½ teaspoon ground nutmeg
1 teaspoon ground cinnamon
⅛ teaspoon sea salt
½ cup chopped pecans
3 cups finely grated carrots

1. Preheat the oven to 350ºF (180ºC). Grease a 13-by-9-inch baking dish with coconut oil.
2. Combine the vanilla extract, maple syrup, and ½ cup of coconut oil in a large bowl. Stir to mix well.
3. Break the eggs in the bowl and whisk to combine well. Set aside. Combine the coconut flour, baking powder, baking soda, nutmeg, cinnamon, and salt in a separate bowl. Stir to mix well. Make a well in the center of the flour mixture, then pour the egg mixture into the well. Stir to combine well. Add the pecans and carrots to the bowl and toss to mix well. Pour the mixture in the single layer on the baking dish. Bake in the preheated oven for 45 minutes or until puffed and the cake spring back when lightly press with your fingers. Remove the cake from the oven. Allow to cool for at least 15 minutes, then serve.

Per Serving

calories: 255 | fat: 21.2g | protein: 5.1g | carbs: 12.8g | fiber: 2.0g | sodium: 202mg

Raspberry Yogurt Basted Cantaloupe

Prep time: 15 minutes | Cook time: 0 minutes | Serves 6

2 cups fresh raspberries, mashed
1 cantaloupe, peeled and sliced
1 cup plain coconut yogurt
½ cup toasted coconut flakes
½ teaspoon vanilla extract

1. Combine the mashed raspberries with yogurt and vanilla extract in a small bowl. Stir to mix well.
2. Place the cantaloupe slices on a platter, then top with raspberry mixture and spread with toasted coconut.
3. Serve immediately.

Per Serving

calories: 75 | fat: 4.1g | protein: 1.2g | carbs: 10.9g | fiber: 6.0g | sodium: 36mg

Apple Compote

Prep time: 15 minutes | Cook time: 10 minutes | Serves 4

6 apples, peeled, cored, and chopped
1 teaspoon ground cinnamon
¼ cup raw honey
¼ cup apple juice
Sea salt, to taste

1. Put all the ingredients in a stockpot. Stir to mix well, then cook over medium-high heat for 10 minutes or until the apples are glazed by honey and lightly saucy. Stir constantly. Serve immediately.

Per Serving

calories: 246 | fat: 0.9g | protein: 1.2g | carbs: 66.3g | fiber: 9.0g | sodium: 62mg

Peanut Butter and Chocolate Balls

Prep time: 45 minutes | Cook time: 0 minutes | Serves 15 balls

¾ cup creamy peanut butter
¼ cup unsweetened cocoa powder
2 tablespoons softened almond butter
½ teaspoon vanilla extract
1¾ cups maple syrup

1. Line a baking sheet with parchment paper.
2. Combine all the ingredients in a bowl. Stir to mix well.
3. Divide the mixture into 15 parts and shape each part into a 1-inch ball. Arrange the balls on the baking sheet and refrigerate for at least 30 minutes, then serve chilled.

Per Serving (1 ball)

calories: 146 | fat: 8.1g | protein: 4.2g | carbs: 16.9g | fiber: 1.0g | sodium: 70mg

Spiced Sweet Pecans

Prep time: 4 minutes | Cook time: 17 minutes | Serves 4

1 cup pecan halves
3 tablespoons almond butter
1 teaspoon ground cinnamon
½ teaspoon ground nutmeg
¼ cup raw honey
¼ teaspoon sea salt

1. Preheat the oven to 350ºF (180ºC). Line a baking sheet with parchment paper.
2. Combine all the ingredients in a bowl. Stir to mix well, then spread the mixture in the single layer on the baking sheet with a spatula. Bake in the preheated oven for 16 minutes or until the pecan halves are well browned.
3. Serve immediately.

Per Serving

calories: 324 | fat: 29.8g | protein: 3.2g | carbs: 13.9g | fiber: 4.0g | sodium: 180mg

Greek Yogurt Affogato with Pistachios

Prep time: 5 minutes | Cook time: 0 minutes | Serves 4

24 ounces (680 g) vanilla Greek yogurt
2 teaspoons sugar
4 shots hot espresso
4 tablespoons chopped unsalted pistachios
4 tablespoons dark chocolate chips

1. Spoon the yogurt into four bowls or tall glasses.
2. Mix ½ teaspoon of sugar into each of the espresso shots.
3. Pour one shot of the hot espresso over each bowl of yogurt.
4. Top each bowl with 1 tablespoon of the pistachios and 1 tablespoon of the chocolate chips and serve.

Per Serving

calories: 190 | fat: 6.0g | protein: 20.0g | carbs: 14.0g | fiber: 1.0g | sodium: 99mg

Grilled Peaches with Whipped Ricotta

Prep time: 5 minutes | Cook time: 14 to 22 minutes | Serves 4

4 peaches, halved and pitted
2 teaspoons extra-virgin olive oil
¾ cup whole-milk Ricotta cheese
1 tablespoon honey
¼ teaspoon freshly grated nutmeg
4 sprigs mint
Cooking spray

1. Spritz a grill pan with cooking spray. Heat the grill pan to medium heat.
2. Place a large, empty bowl in the refrigerator to chill.
3. Brush the peaches all over with the oil. Place half of the peaches, cut-side down, on the grill pan and cook for 3 to 5 minutes, or until grill marks appear.
4. Using tongs, turn the peaches over. Cover the grill pan with aluminum foil and cook for 4 to 6 minutes, or until the peaches are easily pierced with a sharp knife. Set aside to cool. Repeat with the remaining peaches.
5. Remove the bowl from the refrigerator and add the Ricotta. Using an electric beater, beat the Ricotta on high for 2 minutes. Add the honey and nutmeg and beat for 1 more minute. Divide the cooled peaches among 4 serving bowls. Top with the Ricotta mixture and a sprig of mint and serve.

Per Serving

calories: 176 | fat: 8.0g | protein: 8.0g | carbs: 20.0g | fiber: 3.0g | sodium: 63mg

Sauces, Dips, and Dressings

Creamy Cucumber Dip

Prep time: 10 minutes | Cook time: 0 minutes | Serves 6

1 medium cucumber, peeled and grated
¼ teaspoon salt
1 cup plain Greek yogurt
2 garlic cloves, minced
1 tablespoon extra-virgin olive oil
1 tablespoon freshly squeezed lemon juice
¼ teaspoon freshly ground black pepper

1. Place the grated cucumber in a colander set over a bowl and season with salt. Allow the cucumber to stand for 10 minutes. Using your hands, squeeze out as much liquid from the cucumber as possible. Transfer the grated cucumber to a medium bowl.
2. Add the yogurt, garlic, olive oil, lemon juice, and pepper to the bowl and stir until well blended.
3. Cover the bowl with plastic wrap and refrigerate for at least 2 hours to blend the flavors.
4. Serve chilled.

Per Serving (¼ cup)

calories: 47 | fat: 2.8g | protein: 4.2g | carbs: 2.7g | fiber: 0g | sodium: 103mg

Italian Dressing

Prep time: 5 minutes | Cook time: 0 minutes | Serves 12

½ cup extra-virgin olive oil
¼ cup red wine vinegar
1 teaspoon dried Italian seasoning
1 teaspoon Dijon mustard
¼ teaspoon salt
¼ teaspoon freshly ground black pepper
1 garlic clove, minced

1. Place all the ingredients in a mason jar and cover. Shake vigorously for 1 minute until completely mixed.
2. Store in the refrigerator for up to 1 week.

Per Serving (1 tablespoon)

calories: 80 | fat: 8.6g | protein: 0g | carbs: 0g | fiber: 0g | sodium: 51mg

Ranch-Style Cauliflower Dressing

Prep time: 10 minutes | Cook time: 0 minutes | Serves 8

2 cups frozen cauliflower, thawed
½ cup unsweetened plain almond milk
2 tablespoons apple cider vinegar
2 tablespoons extra-virgin olive oil
1 garlic clove, peeled
2 teaspoons finely chopped fresh parsley
2 teaspoons finely chopped scallions (both white and green parts)
1 teaspoon finely chopped fresh dill
½ teaspoon onion powder
½ teaspoon Dijon mustard
½ teaspoon salt
¼ teaspoon freshly ground black pepper

1. Place all the ingredients in a blender and pulse until creamy and smooth.
2. Serve immediately, or transfer to an airtight container to refrigerate for up to 3 days.

Per Serving (2 tablespoons)

calories: 41 | fat: 3.6g | protein: 1.0g | carbs: 1.9g | fiber: 1.1g | sodium: 148mg

Asian-Inspired Vinaigrette

Prep time: 5 minutes | Cook time: 0 minutes | Serves 2

¼ cup extra-virgin olive oil
3 tablespoons apple cider vinegar
1 garlic clove, minced
1 tablespoon peeled and grated fresh ginger
1 tablespoon chopped fresh cilantro
1 tablespoon freshly squeezed lime juice
½ teaspoon sriracha

1. Add all the ingredients in a small bowl and stir to mix well.
2. Serve immediately, or store covered in the refrigerator and shake before using.

Per Serving

calories: 251 | fat: 26.8g | protein: 0g | carbs: 1.8g | fiber: 0.7g | sodium: 3mg

Not Old Bay Seasoning

Prep time: 10 minutes | Cook time: 0 minutes | Makes about ½ cup

3 tablespoons sweet paprika
1 tablespoon mustard seeds
2 tablespoons celery seeds
2 teaspoons freshly ground black pepper
1½ teaspoons cayenne pepper

1 teaspoon red pepper flakes
½ teaspoon ground ginger
½ teaspoon ground nutmeg
½ teaspoon ground cinnamon
¼ teaspoon ground cloves

1. Mix together all the ingredients in an airtight container until well combined.
2. You can store it in a cool, dry, and dark place for up to 3 months.

Per Serving (1 tablespoon)

calories: 26 | fat: 1.9g | protein: 1.1g | carbs: 3.6g | fiber: 2.1g | sodium: 3mg

Tzatziki

Prep time: 15 minutes | Cook time: 0 minutes | Serves 4 to 6

½ English cucumber, finely chopped
1 teaspoon salt, divided
1 cup plain Greek yogurt
8 tablespoons olive oil, divided

1 garlic clove, finely minced
1 to 2 tablespoons chopped fresh dill
1 teaspoon red wine vinegar
½ teaspoon freshly ground black pepper

1. In a food processor, pulse the cucumber until puréed. Place the cucumber on several layers of paper towels lining the bottom of a colander and sprinkle with ½ teaspoon of salt. Allow to drain for 10 to 15 minutes. Using your hands, squeeze out any remaining liquid.
2. In a medium bowl, whisk together the cucumber, yogurt, 6 tablespoons of olive oil, garlic, dill, vinegar, remaining ½ teaspoon of salt, and pepper until very smooth.
3. Drizzle with the remaining 2 tablespoons of olive oil. Serve immediately or refrigerate until ready to serve.

Per Serving

calories: 286 | fat: 29.0g | protein: 3.0g | carbs: 5.0g | fiber: 0g | sodium: 615mg

Harissa Sauce

Prep time: 10 minutes | Cook time: 20 minutes | Makes 3 to 4 cups

1 large red bell pepper, deseeded, cored, and cut into chunks
1 yellow onion, cut into thick rings
4 garlic cloves, peeled
1 cup vegetable broth
2 tablespoons tomato paste
1 tablespoon tamari
1 teaspoon ground cumin
1 tablespoon Hungarian paprika

1. Preheat the oven to 450°F (235°C). Line a baking sheet with parchment paper.
2. Place the bell pepper on the prepared baking sheet, flesh-side up, and space out the onion and garlic around the pepper.
3. Roast in the preheated oven for 20 minutes. Transfer to a blender.
4. Add the vegetable broth, tomato paste, tamari, cumin, and paprika. Purée until smooth. Served chilled or warm.

Per Serving (¼ cup)

calories: 15 | fat: 1.0g | protein: 1.0g | carbs: 3.0g | fiber: 1.0g | sodium: 201mg

Pineapple Salsa

Prep time: 10 minutes | Cook time: 0 minutes | Serves 6 to 8

1 pound (454 g) fresh or thawed frozen pineapple, finely diced, juices reserved
1 white or red onion, finely diced
1 bunch cilantro or mint, leaves only, chopped
1 jalapeño, minced (optional)
Salt, to taste

1. Stir together the pineapple with its juice, onion, cilantro, and jalapeño (if desired) in a medium bowl. Season with salt to taste and serve.
2. The salsa can be refrigerated in an airtight container for up to 2 days.

Per Serving

calories: 55 | fat: 0.1g | protein: 0.9g | carbs: 12.7g | fiber: 1.8g | sodium: 20mg

Garlic Lemon-Tahini Dressing

Prep time: 5 minutes | Cook time: 0 minutes | Serves 8 to 10

½ cup tahini

¼ cup extra-virgin olive oil

¼ cup freshly squeezed lemon juice

1 garlic clove, finely minced

2 teaspoons salt

1. In a glass mason jar with a lid, combine the tahini, olive oil, lemon juice, garlic, and salt. Cover and shake well until combined and creamy.
2. Store in the refrigerator for up to 2 weeks.

Per Serving

calories: 121 | fat: 12.0g | protein: 2.0g | carbs: 3.0g | fiber: 1.0g | sodium: 479mg

Creamy Grapefruit and Tarragon Dressing

Prep time: 5 minutes | Cook time: 0 minutes | Serves 4 to 6

½ cup avocado oil mayonnaise

2 tablespoons Dijon mustard

1 teaspoon dried tarragon or 1 tablespoon chopped fresh tarragon

½ teaspoon salt

Zest and juice of ½ grapefruit

¼ teaspoon freshly ground black pepper

1 to 2 tablespoons water (optional)

1. In a large mason jar with a lid, combine the mayonnaise, Dijon, tarragon, grapefruit zest and juice, salt, and pepper and whisk well with a fork until smooth and creamy. If a thinner dressing is preferred, thin out with water.
2. Serve immediately or refrigerate until ready to serve.

Per Serving

calories: 86 | fat: 7.0g | protein: 1.0g | carbs: 6.0g | fiber: 0g | sodium: 390mg

Alphabetical Index

Printed in Great Britain
by Amazon